THE SALMON FISHERMAN'S YEAR

The Salmon Fisherman's Year

Crawford Little

LOCHAR PUBLISHING · MOFFAT · SCOTLAND

© Crawford Little, 1990
Published by Lochar Publishing Ltd
MOFFAT DG10 9JU

British Library Cataloguing in Publication Data
Little, Crawford
The salmon fisherman's year.
1. Great Britain. Salmon & trout. Angling
I. Title
799.1755

ISBN 0-948403-46-2

Typeset in Cheltenham 10/12 point by Novatext Graphix, Edinburgh
Printed by
Scotprint, Musselburgh

Contents

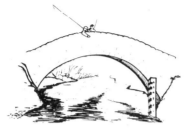

AN EARLY SEASON SALMON – THE FIRST FISH OF THE SEASON IS PRIZED ABOVE ALL OTHERS, PARTICULARLY WHEN, AS IN THIS CASE, IT IS TAKEN ON FLY.

CHAPTER ONE

January

FIRST FISH OF THE SEASON

Just look at this beautiful fish with its ebony back, silvery flanks tinged with pink and blue, and its creamy-rich, white belly. . . . Such salmon remain far clearer in my memory than any number of summer fish taken on the floating line.

The sharp-toothed, northerly wind dragged at the tip of my long rod, still secure in its clamps on the roof of my car. The green sinking line strummed like loose rigging on a sailing ship. Only a fool would forsake the warmth and comfort of his bed so early on such a wild and blustery, late-January morning. The gillie would not arrive for another 10 minutes, so, with nothing else to do, I walked the few yards down to the hump-backed stone bridge that carries the shore road across the steep-sided glen.

The view over the bridge parapet carried across the lowermost of the river's freshwater pools, over the tidal sea-pool, across the estuary and out to the open sea. There, hustled on by impatient squalls, the wind showed its awesome power. Far out in the firth, a dirty little coaster plunged her bows through wall after wall of foaming sea. I wondered what cargo for the remote Isles had encouraged her skipper and crew out of safe harbour in such conditions.

Seagulls wheeled in the brave boat's wake. They soared before a background of snow-dusted hills and stark white peaks silhouetted against the black sky. The blood of generations of seafarers in my veins, watching the gulls as they called in a lonely sky, I thought of the souls of lost sailors; of those in peril on the sea.

The boat bobbed up out of the foaming sea. The wet-lipped wind brought a stinging flurry of sleet. I pulled up the collar of my tweed coat and crouched in the lee of the bridge parapet.

"Aye, it's a grand day for the fishing!"

The sound of my gillie's arrival in his old van had been carried away on the wind.

"That's just what I was thinking. We must be mad!", I replied. "Why on earth do we do it?"

He had no need to say. Those of the salmon fishing calling who have shown themselves prepared to take up the gauntlet thrown down by a Highland winter, with its short days of cutting winds, snow and icy water, know the reasons why. We seek the reward of that deep, slow and, oh, so thrilling tug of a taking salmon: The first salmon of a new season; the salmon we know as springers.

Who was he who first thought to talk of 'springers' and 'spring fishing' during the opening months of the season? Whoever he was, he must have had a strangely complex and twisted mind. Spring fishing, indeed! There will be no delightfully warm days for a good, long while. No hosts of golden daffodils or frolicking lambs will gladden the countryside. The 'spring' salmon-fisher must face facts and be prepared for bone-chilling gales, when hands, face and feet lose all sensation but the bitter bite of cold. I have suffered the sheer agonies of returning circulation at the end of a day when I forgot to don mittens, scarf and woolly hat. But so what? The first springer of the season is the finest salmon of them all.

Just look at this beautiful fish with its ebony back, silvery flanks tinged with pink and blue, and its creamy-rich, white belly. What a prize! But springers are hard-found. The spring runs have diminished in nearly all rivers. Few of them are worth fishing until much later in the season. Some rivers are not open until February or later. January, February and March all see salmon fishermen travelling the high roads to rivers whose very names ring with the splendour of fishing glories: Helmsdale and Brora, Carron, Oykel, and Shin.

Classic salmon rivers such as Spey, Dee, Tay and Tweed still have numbers of spring salmon, but they are virtually as nothing compared to the stocks of times past. Fishing effort is concentrated on the lower beats. Much of the activity is with spinning rods, and boats are out to harl the Tay. Well, one man's meat is another man's poison. While I still take a turn with the spinning rod, I far prefer to take my salmon on the fly.

More and more fishermen are thinking along these lines. Some spend the closed season dreaming of a cast on the Piper's, Long Pool or Shoulder of Cromartie below the Falls of Shin. Others find their minds turning to thoughts of pools below Kildonan Falls on the Helmsdale. Perhaps they picture Upper and Lower Caen, the Sand, the Alder, and the Stall on Number One Beat Below; or dream of the 300 yards of excellent water in Kilphedir, or perhaps of Upper Torrish? It was in Upper Torrish that a 45-pounder was hooked. It ran three miles upstream during the three hours in which it was fought and finally beaten. And then there are really great spring pools on Number Six Beat Below: the Dyke, Church, Manse, Little and Big Rock. . . . But no more digressing. Let's away back to the river where I fished during that last week of January. . . .

Salmon are in no great hurry to run during the opening months of the season. The open sea retains a reservoir of warmth throughout the winter, with the water temperature rarely falling below the lower 40s. For the salmon, the transition from the relatively warm sea to a river, where the temperature may be barely above freezing, may be likened to a man dipping his toe in a cold bath. Well, the analogy may be rather far-stretched, but, certainly, until the river temperature starts to approach that of the sea, which may not happen until well into March or even April, fishing prospects can hardly be described as good for the fly-fisherman. Until the water temperature of the river exceeds 42 degrees Fahrenheit, the salmon will normally just nose their way into the lower pools and stretches and be halted downstream of any obstruction.

These early-season springers are, however, really fresh fish. I think that is why, despite their being thin on the ground, they are generally not too difficult to catch: not too difficult, that is, so long as the fly is chosen wisely and craftily presented at a suitable angle, speed and depth. There lies the rub. In all this talk of 'not too difficult', the fact is that the fly-fisher often experiences considerable problems in that search to swim an appropriate fly in a productive style. It is simple in theory, difficult in practice. And, in an early-season blow, the necessarily powerful rod and heavy, sinking line can be beasts to work with.

Kit for early-season fly-fishing should be as simple and straightforward as possible. I see no point in fiddling about with gadgetry when the hands are numbed with cold, or in wishing for a longer, stronger rod when I'm rolling a deeply-sunk line up to the surface ready to be punched out with a double Spey cast into the teeth of a nor'easter. A rod of 15 ft or longer is best for this class of work, and a good, powerful one at that. It must have plenty of back-bone, and it is best coupled to an utterly uncomplicated and foolproof, large-diameter, single-action fly-reel. Two lines, a medium-fast and a very fast sinker, both full-length, double-tapers, serve well.

A medium-sinker such as the Wet-Col 2, described in fact as a fast-sinker by its manufacturers, has plenty of scope for fishing at sufficient depth in most places, just so long as it is fished slowly enough. You can hardly fish your fly too slowly when salmon are apparently anaesthetised in near-freezing water. At such times, until the water temperature has struggled up into the 40s, most salmon are lying in the deep, slow dubs of the pools, and it is here, in particular, that the medium-sinker can be productive. There are times, however, when the fish are in the slack 'curtain' at the side of a heavy push of water over which the fly must be cast before it is swum back over the fish. Here, a very fast sinker will cut through the stream to emerge into the slack water at sufficient depth to interest a resting salmon. Remember the general rule that, until the water temperature has risen considerably, an 'eyeball-to-eyeball' confrontation should be sought between fly and fish, the offering served as if on a plate, so that the salmon has only to ease forward in the take.

On to each of my own lines is needle-knotted about 18 inches of 30 lb nylon, finished with a loop. A short leader is then attached 'loop-to-loop' as shown in the accompanying 'Fisherman's Knot' illustration. The leader is 4–5 ft of 20 lb nylon. Strong leaders are in keeping with the rest of the tackle, the conditions to be met, and the flies that are normally chosen.

Generations of fishing experience have shown that cold-water conditions normally demand that not only should the fly be fished slow and deep, but that it should be tied on the generous side. Once upon a time, such flies were tied on enormous single hooks, up to 10/0. Today, most British fishermen have voted firmly in favour of the modern generation of articulated flies.

They are called 'articulated' because the hook is separate from the part of the fly carrying the body-dressing and wing. Hence, articulated, as in lorries. Armed with a relatively small treble hook, and avoiding the leverage of a long shank on the hook-hold, they may be considered as the 'state of the art' in terms of hooking and holding salmon on long flies.

Articulated flies come in three main types. The most common is the tube-fly. The tube on which the fly is dressed, can be of plastic, aluminium, copper or brass, according to the sinking-rate desired. The leader is threaded through the tube and tied to a suitable size of treble hook held in line with the tube in a short length of flexible extension tubing. The second options uses the style of shank attributed to Richard Waddington. This is eyed and offers positive attachments, at one end for the leader and at the other for the treble. However, Waddingtons are, in my opinion, just a little too light for many cold-water fishing conditions, when it is reassuring to know that the fly is settling down in the water and fishing at about the same level as the sunk fly-line.

The third option is really nothing more than a beefed-up version of the Waddington double-shank. Rob Wilson, who has now retired from his tackle-shop in Brora, was the first to offer a commercial solution to the weight problem that some of us felt was inherent in Waddingtons under some conditions. He simply had the shanks produced in a heavier gauge of stainless steel wire. These flies came to be known as 'Broras'.

Allied to the new generation of highly successful cold-water salmon patterns, such as the magnificent Willie Gunn, Pilkington, Black-and-yellow, Spey Royal and the like, here is a design and a series of flies that has earned the affection of large numbers of salmon fishermen from Thurso to Tweed. The Waddington-style shank can be fished in partnership with such flies as a lightweight alternative when circumstances dictate.

Making the choice between tube-flies or Brora- or Waddington-style patterns can be quite complicated. I carry all three types. Now and again I have a few niggles about tube-flies. For one thing, a tube has nothing to protect the relatively soft metal at its front end when it is fished deep and inevitably, sometimes grazes on sharp rocks. On more than one occasion, I have found the head of tube has become jagged and pinched hard on to the leader. Nylon tubing inserted into a metal tube helps to alleviate the problem, but is far from being a complete solution.

On the other hand, tubes are excellent in that they offer the minimum of leverage on the hook-hold. A tube slides up the leader away from the treble, just as a Devon minnow does. And tubes are so convenient, as well as being more economic in terms of the number of expensive trebles which have to be attached to each and every Waddington- and Brora-style fly. At the end of the day, you pays your money and you takes your choice.

But let's get back to the river. . . .

The gillie led me upstream from the bridge. We walked in single file through the old, rank heather on a narrow path that avoided the worst of the jumbles of rocks and boulders that litter the river-bank on the way up to the Falls Pool.

Falls Pool is usually a good bet at this time of year. Salmon do not ascend the falls until the water temperature is in the 40s. Of course, the fish do not simply swim into the pool below the falls and wait for warmer times. They spread themselves back over a fair distance and through a number of pools. Thus we tend on this stretch to pace the fishing day, so that having made a start at the top, we can fish downstream through each pool, missing out the thinner water that cannot really be expected to hold fish at this time of season, and then have just enough time to nip back up to give Falls Pool a last try in the fading light of dusk.

Long Pool, just below the bridge, is another grand holding pool. My own choice is to be at its head and lengthening line to start fishing it down at about midday.

Midday on the Long Pool, dusk on the Falls. . . . In low water conditions in summer, dawn and dusk are often the best taking times for salmon. Keen fishermen may make a start with dusk salmon, fish through the night for sea-trout, then have a final try for the bigger fish before tumbling into bed just as others are wakening. But, in the opening and closing cold-water months of the season, it is the middle hours of the day, together with the dusk, which often see maximum activity on the salmon river.

Winter days are all too short. It's as well to have a fly in the water by 10 am – there is little point in fishing earlier – and then to fish through to about 2.30 pm, stopping then for a mug of soup and a sandwich and returning to fish until the last of the light has gone.

In the Falls, the mainstream curves below the sheer rock face of the opposite bank. The salmon, if any are up, will normally be lying in midstream and about half-way down the pool, or back in the glide. Having pitched the fly as close as possible to the opposite bank, the angler's problem is to get line and fly to cut down through the heavy stream. A long, accurate, and shallow-angled cast is needed to give the line time to sink and reach a fishable depth

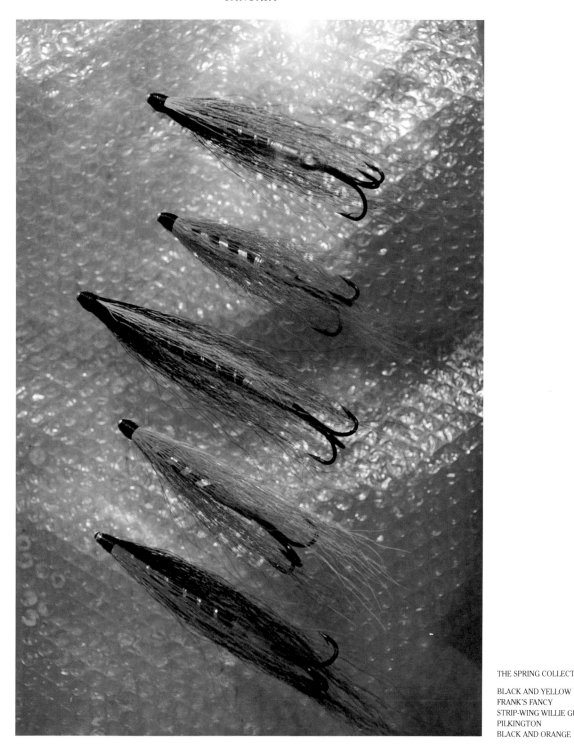

THE SPRING COLLECTION – TOP TO BOTTOM:

BLACK AND YELLOW
FRANK'S FANCY
STRIP-WING WILLIE GUNN
PILKINGTON
BLACK AND ORANGE

before the fly covers the fish. Wading in at the head of the pool in spring is cold work, but it is the necessary means to the end of tempting a fish into taking. Now, as much as at any other time of the season, the angler's thoughts should be on the angle, speed and depth at which his fly is fishing. All sorts of tricks can be tried to keep in firm control and to have the fly swim attractively across the fish.

Incidentally, if anyone is confused by my saying 'fish' instead of salmon, they will have to excuse my Scottish ways. In Scotland there is but one fish, and that fish, or *fush* as it tends to be pronounced, is the salmon. Thus a cod is a cod and a trout a trout, but a *fush* is always a salmon. So there we are.

Many fishermen see a heavy fly as a means of achieving the desired depth, and especially those brass tubes that have been said to come in three types: 'heavy, very heavy, and damned ridiculous'. Even more ridiculous, to my mind at least, are those so called 'super-heavy' brass tubes with an overlay of lead wire. Such flies are difficult to cast and dangerous to boot. There is no chance of their fishing effectively and swimming attractively except in the heaviest of currents, where fish will not be lying anyway. One wonders whether the users of such flies are at all interested in the niceties of whether fish are hooked in the mouth, back or flank.

My own preference is for a lighter fly, and with tubes there is seldom any need to go heavier than the standard copper tube and the aluminium alternative is often useful. Such relatively light flies can be taken down to the required depth by altering the sinking rate of the line. This, I believe, follows the best ethics of cold-water fly-fishing.

I shun the use of shooting-heads. No fisherman who has taken the trouble to master the roll-cast and Spey cast need use any line other than a double-taper. Shooting-heads may be all right for fishing from a boat on a fat lower river beat, but not for the more usual wading. What pleasure is achieved from getting yourself entangled, and fiddling about with yard upon yard of shooting line?

Incidentally, don't believe those who say that you cannot Spey-cast a sinking line. Once a roll-cast has been made to bring a sunk line to the surface, then you can go straight into any cast you wish.

The double-Spey is arguably best for ease and safety with sinking lines and large flies, but the single-Spey can be used if the wind is blowing upstream. It may be true that you cannot Spey-cast a sinking line that is sunk, but you can Spey-cast a sinking line that has been rolled up to the surface.

This is where a long rod comes into its own. Rods of 15–17ft will roll, lift and throw great lengths of line, even if a good oath and a bit of a bash are needed to punch out the line into a stiff breeze. . . .

Nothing moved to my fly in the Falls Pool, nor on the other two pools covered before noon. By 12.20 pm we were left at the tail of the Long Pool below the bridge. I remember the time because I looked at my watch to see if I had enough time to fish it through again. It is a great holding pool at the start of the season and in most heights of water, and it had looked so 'fishy' as we approached it that I was a little disappointed not to have so much as moved a fish.

First time down, normal practice is to try to keep fly fishing effectively by casting at a fairly square angle and hand-lining it back. This pool would not do for a man who sees salmon water only in terms of great beats on classic rivers, where the current is nearly always sufficient to swim the fly effectively without any interference from the fisherman. No, the Long Pool is slow-moving. In fact, it is almost canal-like.

Realising that time was on my side, I cast squarely again and gave line and fly a few seconds to settle into the water before I walked upstream for three paces and retrieved a few yards more hand-lining. Then cast again and repeated the process, backing-up toward the head of the pool.

Backing-up sounds all wrong, doesn't it? However, it causes the fly to swim purposefully across the resting places of the fish. A fast-sinking line used with a really light fly – perhaps a plastic tube – causes the fly to rise slowly and then surge down over the fish's head.

We usually associate cold-water salmon with slow-motion takes. We think of an unhurried, steady tightening of the line. Backing-up can provoke a much stronger response.

Halfway back up the pool, with the fly swimming strongly across in midstream, a salmon took with a real *bang!* The fish backed-off downstream, like a terrier worrying at a scarf. The line retrieved during the backing-up had soon been drawn away by the fish, and I could breathe a sigh of relief and set about playing it off the reel. Then the salmon, untypically for a springer, leapt and leapt again in a shower of spray before running hard across the pool.

The hook-hold might have torn during those two unexpected leaps. Perhaps the gillie was also worried, but he didn't say. However, all was well. The fish has sucked the 2-inch Willie Gunn deep into its throat. In fact we had to cut out the stout treble hook.

What a marvellous way to open the season! A beautifully fresh fish of 14 lb, short for its weight, but high in the shoulder. He shone silver-clean beneath the ebony of his topsides. But I would have plenty more time to admire him later. Winter days are too short to be spent in long sessions of self-congratulation.

We fished down the next two pools with the same combination of standard downstream technique followed by backing-up, but nothing was doing. The next pool was blank, too, and the tide was wrong for the Sea Pool, so we hurried on back to fish the Falls at the top of the beat.

With little more than half-an-hour's fishing light left, I tied on a 2½-inch Whitewing and was straight in at the head of the pool while the gillie sought shelter in which to stoke and light his pipe. Casting was far from easy. Most winds fade or die altogether with the approach of dusk. Today, the wind continued to gather strength, as it had throughout the day. My language was becoming fairly choice. Nothing, absolutely nothing, is so effective or satisfying as a mighty oath to lift a line off the water and punch it into the teeth of a wind!

The light had all but gone. My arms were weary, and my mind was locked into thoughts of relaxing in a deep, hot bath with only a dram for company. But the gillie insisted that we should give it just five minutes more. Fourth cast down, the salmon took in a long, slow draw before hammering into the mainstream and down into the tail of the pool. It was just a whisker more than 8 lb, a nice fish, typical of the spring run, and just right for the table.

Such days and salmon remain far clearer in my memory than any number of summer fish taken on the floating line. Success is infinitely more enjoyable in the face of such a challenge and so little expectation. Two fresh springers in one day's fishing with the fly is great sport, and a real red-letter day in my fishing diary. I have fished a whole week for less. But even when cold, tired and fishless, one has satisfaction from fishing the fly and meeting the challenge. Equally, there is nothing like a springer on the bank to make the whole thing worthwhile!

FISHERMAN'S KNOTS

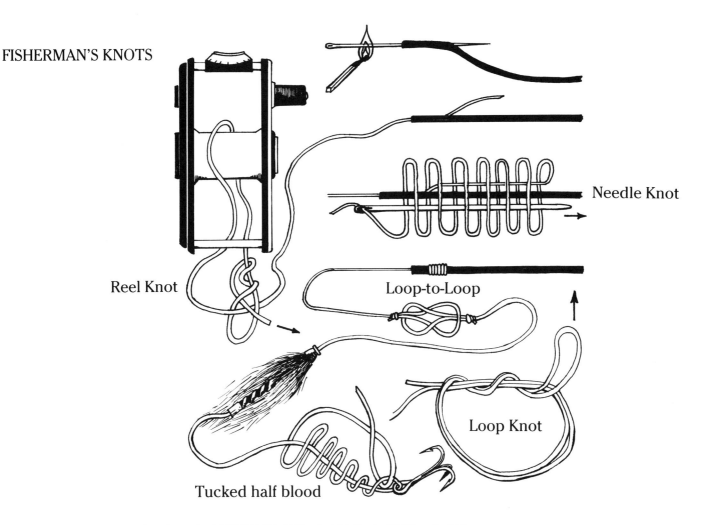

Needle Knot

Reel Knot

Loop-to-Loop

Loop Knot

Tucked half blood

The salmon: Fish tend to be lethargic and reluctant to travel far until the river temperature is the same or greater than the sea's, which does not normally occur until March. They will not ascend obstacles until the water temperature exceeds 42 degrees Fahrenheit. They are most active around noon and at dusk.

Tackle: The outfit should be as simple and ruggedly powerful as the fisherman can handle in comfort. Rods should be 15–17 ft class, with plenty of backbone to handle the double-taper fast-sinking lines.

Flies: Articulated flies are used – tubes, Waddingtons or 'Brora-style' wire shanks. Popular patterns include Willie Gunn, Pilkington, Frank's Fancy, Black-and-orange or Spey Royal, Black-and-yellow, Orange-and-yellow, Garry and so on.

Technique: Concentrate on fishing the fly deep and slow in the slower, deeper parts of recognised holding pools.

CHAPTER TWO

February

SPRINGERS, SPINNER AND FLIES

While casts of 30 yards and more are possible with long carbon fly-rods, it is equally true that a long carbon spinning rod and modern multiplier reel will hurl a big Toby more than twice that distance. On larger rivers this can make all the difference between success and failure.

Somebody once said to me that he presumed that I must be a 'fly-only' fisherman. I told him he was wrong, but when I look back over what I have written about the pursuit of salmon, and see that it is almost totally dominated by discussions of sport with the fly, I can see why he made his mistake. But it was a mistake, because despite the fact that natural bait fishing in now long behind me, these are still times and places that, to my mind, cry out for the spinner.

Having said that, it also has to be said that it is some time since I have used anything other than a fly-rod! I enjoy using a fly-rod so much more than any of its alternatives, so I fish it whenever and wherever I can. I do not see its almost exclusive use as any sort of a limitation. If I did, I would not keep with it quite so loyally.

Twenty years ago, however, most of my salmon were taken by spinning. So what has changed?

The last two decades have seen some fundamental changes of thought on the catching of salmon. Many have come about in such a subtle manner that we hardly notice, for example, that cold-water salmon-fishing conventions have been so seriously questioned.

Twenty years ago, few gillies would have been impressed by your trying to fish fly in the opening months of the season, unless you were forced to do so by a 'fly-only' rule. Spinning was the method to use until water temperature had risen into the 40s. Then it was to try the sinking line and large fly until the water temperature was into the 50s, when floating line and small-fly tactics took over. This strong tradition still persists on many salmon rivers, and many anglers still believe that much can be said in its favour.

Nowadays, however, the big difference is that more and more fishermen are prepared to fish fly even in the lowest temperatures. This has been made possible only by advances in tackle. Twenty years ago, when I was in my late teens, the Spey cast was considered rather unconventional. Equally, we thought that fibre-glass rods could hardly be improved upon. And we did not have the great range of alternative sinking fly-lines that we have today.

Now, due almost exclusively to the advent of carbon-fibre rods, a great revival of interest in the Spey cast has been awakened. Roll a sunk line on to the surface of the water, and you can do virtually what you like with it: punch it out with a single-Spey if the wind is gusting upstream, or the double-Spey if the wind is downstream. It is as easy as pie once you have learned, practised and got the hang of the timing needed. A polished performer with a 15 ft or longer carbon rod can put out the entire length of a standard fly-line. Longer lines have been introduced to allow rods of 17 ft and more to be used to their full potential. Carbon rods, Spey-casting and a range of sinking lines have revolutionised our approach to cold-water salmon-fishing, allowing us to achieve distances, angles, speeds and depths of presentation which previously we could achieve only with the spinning rod.

Then we have the modern generation of salmon flies. Twenty years ago, articulated flies, while having already gained an immense reputation, were virtually in their infancy. Today, some anglers will still fish through the cold-water months with nothing more than a 2-inch Willie Gunn on a copper tube. I can relate with their attitude. The Willie Gunn, on its day, is a peerless fly pattern and design, but we do have worthwhile alternatives. Twenty years ago, a pattern such as the long-winged Collie Dog would have been written-off as totally impractical by all but a few of the more eccentric salmon fishermen. Who first thought to tie an immensely long wing on a relatively short hook, and then had the cheek to swim it in a salmon river? Thank goodness for such eccentrics!

Then there are those autumn salmon that I so enjoy catching on flies tied on relatively short copper tubes and short Brora shanks fished on an intermediate or slow-sinking line. Such tactics and tackle also serve well in spring, say late April or early May, when the temperature is between 45 and 50 degrees Farenheit. This is the sunk-line fishing that I firmly associate with relatively shallow pools in perfect ply – pools that contain a great variety of resting lies for salmon and where you can cast and virtually forget about your fly until it has swum round on to the dangle. It is a method that goes perfectly with the technique of striking off the reel, for it involves no hand-lining until the closing moments of fishing out the cast. Oh, my mind goes back to the great days of sport with the long rod!

An intermediate line is usually palely visible beneath the surface, and I like one that settles just below the surface and fishes the fly a foot or so down. Sure, this is cold water, but it is not too cold for a salmon in taking mood to come up to intercept a 1½-inch Brora. A range of tubes and Broras up to about 3 inches can be fished in a spirit of co-operation with rather than competition against long-winged flies such as the Collie Dog. If one doesn't work; then the other may. And the whole task is doubly satisfying when the reel sings.

While such tactics have grown out of traditional salmon-fishing practices, their development owes much to recent developments in tackle. They provide a stimulus that would not be as well presented with spinning tackle, whatever the champions of the 2-inch black-and-gold Devon minnow may have said in the past.

Trends in warm-water fishing techniques, and the reasons behind them, tend to reflect what has been happening in cold-water techniques. For example, the technique of mending line, which involves rolling a loop of line up or downstream to control the speed, angle and depth of the fly, tends to be disregarded by the modern deep-wading fishermen, who can throw great lengths of line with their long carbon rods and Spey casts. They rely instead on a relatively shallow-angled cast, well downstream, to ensure that the fly does not swing across the stream too quickly. This may be viewed as a tactical error; or at least as a denial of what can be a useful ace up your sleeve. It does not make good fishing sense to mend line habitually, whatever the circumstances. Neither is it sense to ignore a technique which, when used thoughtfully, can give a clear tactical advantage.

Mending line when necessary, coupled with the ability to throw a long line and wade deep, gives tremendous advantages. With modern carbon rods almost anyone is able to throw a longer line than did his predecessors. I remember the late John Ashley Cooper being adamant in telling me that the ability to cast a long line – and he was talking about casts in excess of 30 yds – put any fisherman at a tremendous advantage on big rivers such as Spey and Ness.

But we cannot all be Ashley Coopers. Better to view the 30-yd cast as something to be aimed for, and to be not too dispirited if it isn't achieved. A cast of 29 yds will do nicely.

Much of the evolution of modern sunk-line fishing would not have occurred had it not been for the introduction of the carbon-fibre rods. Nothing like as many fishermen would have been putting aside their spinning rods had we not progressed beyond cane. In changing from cane to glass and then to carbon-fibre, most of us have added perhaps 3 ft to the length of our rods and as much as 10 yds to our casting range. We are able to handle far more line, with much greater control, than was ever possible in the past. It is our greater control of depth, speed and angle of presentation that has proved so effective and virtually revolutionised so many fishermen's attitudes to the sunk line. We shall always find situations that provide exceptions to the rule, but, for myself, I just cannot find any sensible answer to the question: "Why spin where and when you can fish the fly?"

But what about those exceptions to the rule, those places where we *cannot* fish fly effectively? There, I believe, the spinning rod will remain the first choice when its major capabilities, which I call 'The Three D's' – depth, distance, dominance – are needed.

No one can deny that the spinning rod is the most efficient tool for fishing a lure at any depth greater than, say, 6 ft. To fish a fly at such depth on a fly-rod is sheer hard work. If this point seems difficult to believe, just try to fish some of the deep, chasm-sided pools on the Cumbrian Eden early in the season.

Similarly, while casts of 30 yds and more are possible with long carbon fly-rods, it is equally true that a long carbon spinning rod and modern multiplier reel will hurl a big Toby more than twice that distance! On larger rivers, such as lower Spey or Dee, this can put the fisherman at a tremendous advantage. On a river such as the Tay, it can literally make all the difference between success and failure.

Put a good fly-caster – a man who can cast a 30 yd line – on the bank of a biggish river and tell him to make his normally angled cast, and his fly will land no more than 20 yds from the bank. Tell him to wade and he may reach 10 yds from the bank, so now his fly will pitch 30 yds out. Let him do the same from the other bank and cover a 30 yd strip down that side. Even a really accomplished fly-caster, with modern tackle, and who is prepared to wade deep, will be unable to cover all of the pool unless it is no more than 60 yds wide. And many pools can be fished off only one bank, with a boat not always available.

So that is depth and distance dealt with. Dominance is the last of my 'Three D's', and this is what might be called the 'crunch' factor. Spinning tackle gives an angler the ability to dominate contrary wind conditions. We can *all* be beaten with fly-tackle – and be in some physical danger – when a gale is blowing straight into our faces, or else we are so severely limited in our casting range that, on medium-to-large rivers, unless the river is in spate, and

A SELECTION OF EARLY SEASON SPINNERS AND SPOONS. DEVON MINNOWS ARE ONE OF THE MOST POPULAR SPINNING BAITS FOR SALMON. AND ARE PARTICULARLY USEFUL FOR FISHING DEEP, SLOW WATER. THE TOBY IS BEST IN FASTER STREAMS.

we are virtually dangling a fly down the bank, we are forced to stop fishing. With a spinning rod, while we might curse a bit, we would still be able to bang-out a reasonable length of line – and in safety.

These three factors govern my thinking about spinning when; I am unable to reach the required depth with standard fly tackle; or I am unable to cover all the water (when I will fish the closer lies with a fly, but cover mid-stream by other means); or I am sick and tired of trying to punch out a fly-line into the teeth of a gale.

This represents my personal thinking, but, please, never dismiss the spinning rod if: you never fish really deep rivers; you never fish really big rivers; and you head for the fishing hut when the wind really starts to blow.

Bearing in mind my discussions of dominance, distance and depth no one should be surprised to learn that my spinning gear is chosen from the more powerful end of the range!

One firm preference is for a multiplier reel. A multiplier feels right for long-distance casting with heavy weights. A fixed-spool reel isn't really in the same league when it comes to hurling heavy lures over wide, open stretches of water, where 60-yd casts are the order of the day and accuracy takes a back-seat. A big spoon, such as a 1 oz Toby, will fly out like a bullet, and you can drop to little more than $\frac{1}{2}$ oz and still cope reasonably well. The multiplier is a winner all the way in terms of fish-fighting ability.

But multipliers are not cheap, and a top-of-the-range model may cost close to a three-figure sum. Anyone who does little spinning may find it hard to justify spending such a sum – unless, of course, he also does a lot of sea fishing.

My own two (of three) Abu multipliers are excellent tools for salmon, as well as for inshore sea fishing. They are a 6500C and an XLT 3 with what is described as 'Syncrodrag'. It frightened me to start with, but now it is my faithful companion on beach and boat! Both reels have identical capacities – about 200 yds of 15 lb line; which is ideal for any British salmon fishing that I may encounter. My third reel is a 7000C, which I would take if I were to fish in Norway. (They do still allow spinning on some of their rivers, don't they?) I could squeeze 200 yds of 30 lb, or nearly 300 yds of 20 lb on to this reel. Failing Norway, it will continue to handle cod, pollack and tope.

My choice of 15 lb nylon may seem light, to some people. However, apart from the fact that any beach-caster will tell you that 15 lb is about ideal for casting from a 6500C, it has landed some big fish for me in high, heavy water on big rivers without ever giving cause for concern. But you must buy good-quality nylon. Let's not forget that Callum Gillies, a well-known gillie, was using 15 lb nylon when he landed three salmon for a total weight in excess of 100 lb in the course of a morning.

I realise that in choosing to spin with a multiplier, I really should search out a crank-handled rod. Meantime, I am happy to use a standard, double-hander, just so long as it is no shorter than 10 ft. I do like long spinning rods, and I hope I may be excused for saying that they allow a spinner to be fished like a fly – yes, even to the extent of bringing the lure on to the dangle and then leading it across. A short, stiff rod is too lacking in response and cushioning in playing a fish. I even have a 12 ft carbon spinning rod for use when extreme casting range or prolonged hanging the lure are needed. No other spinning rod I have ever handled has come so close to matching the feel of a fly-rod when a salmon is at the end of the line. Incidentally, rods seem all to be designed for use with fixed-spool reels. A multiplier is fished on top of a rod, so it may need to be re-ringed, or at least have a ring or two added, to

THE AUTHOR STILL ENJOYS A SESSION WITH THE SPINNING ROD, WHEN CONDITIONS DEMAND ITS USE. THE SPINNING ROD INCREASES CASTING RANGE, FISHES A LURE AT DEPTH TO GREAT EFFECT, AND IS NOT AFFECTED BY CONTRARY WINDS THAT WOULD BE DIFFICULT OR DANGEROUS TO THE FLY FISHER.

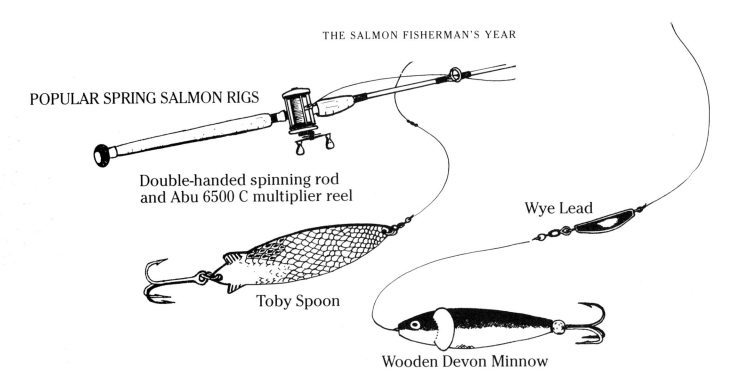

POPULAR SPRING SALMON RIGS

Double-handed spinning rod
and Abu 6500 C multiplier reel

Wye Lead

Toby Spoon

Wooden Devon Minnow

keep the line off the blank when a fish is being played.

I will not even start to describe the rest of my spinning gear, and the methods of fishing it. Suffice that I have said enough to remind myself, at least, that I am not a 'fly-only' man after all . . . but very nearly.

FLY VERSUS SPINNER
When a spinning rod becomes the logical choice

Distance: On big, wide rivers such as the Tay, lower Spey and lower Dee, it may not be possible to cover the entire water effectively with a fly-rod without resorting to a boat.

Depth: Spinning tackle is very efficient for fishing a lure at greater depths than the fly. This is particularly relevant to rivers with deep, chasm-sided pools.

Dominance: With a spinning rod, any contrary wind become nothing more than a nuisance, whereas with a fly-rod, the situation can become either unmanageable or downright dangerous.

Diversity: There are times when we give the fly-rod our best, but it simply does not produce the goods. This tends to happen in particular when our water temperature is below 40 degrees Fahrenheit. The spinner or spoon offers an alternative stimulus.

Tackle: The author prefers longer spinning rods: up to 12 ft and never less than 10 ft early in the season. More effort is needed in learning how to handle a multiplier reel, but, loaded with a 15 lb or 16 lb nylon, it is highly effective for long-range, heavy spinning.

CHAPTER THREE

March

IN PRAISE OF LONG-WINGED FLIES

On rivers great and small, these long-winged flies have shimmered and shimmied their way into our fishing experience. Indeed, their success on some Highland rivers has been so marked for some fishermen that they seldom fish anything else.

I t wasn't so much the bonny little springer that had just been grassed that caught my eye as the fly which had taken it. A hank of long hair – and I do mean long – cut from the feathering on the hind-leg of a working collie was lashed to the bare shank of an aluminium tube. This was my introduction to the Collie Dog fly. So now I knew what it looked like and, yes, that it did catch fish.

I did wonder at the time whether that fish did any more than prove the old gillie's saying: "There's aye a daft one aboot," because according to all the accepted lores of salmon fishing, any self-respecting salmon should either have ignored the fly entirely or simply tugged at the long, trailing 'wing' and missed the hook. It all seemed so wildly improbable. Who in his right mind would fish a fly with a 6-inch wing on a $1^{1}/_{2}$-inch tube?

The answer now is that lots of us would, and do, because we have learned to think differently. On rivers great and small, from the classiest of private beats to the lowliest of hard-fished public waters, these long-winged flies have shimmered and shimmied their way into our fishing experience. Collies and the like have caught countless salmon. Indeed, their success on Highland rivers has been so marked for some fishermen that they seldom fish anything else. It is all the more intriguing because this new generation of flies has brought into question so much that we once took for granted.

Long-wings have shown that some of the foundations on which we build our traditional approach to salmon, particularly in cold water, are just a little shaky, and they offer some real and useful alternatives.

Not everybody agrees as to the worth of long-wings. I was certainly a doubter – until I saw such flies in use. It is, however, a great shame that some still choose either to ignore or to twist the evidence set before them.

The season after my initial introduction to long-winged patterns, brought an invitation to fish another Highland river. The time was late March. My hopes were high for success with the sinking line and standard articulated patterns. I dreamed of perfect March conditions, with the river falling and clearing after a spate, and the water temperature in the lower 40s Fahrenheit.

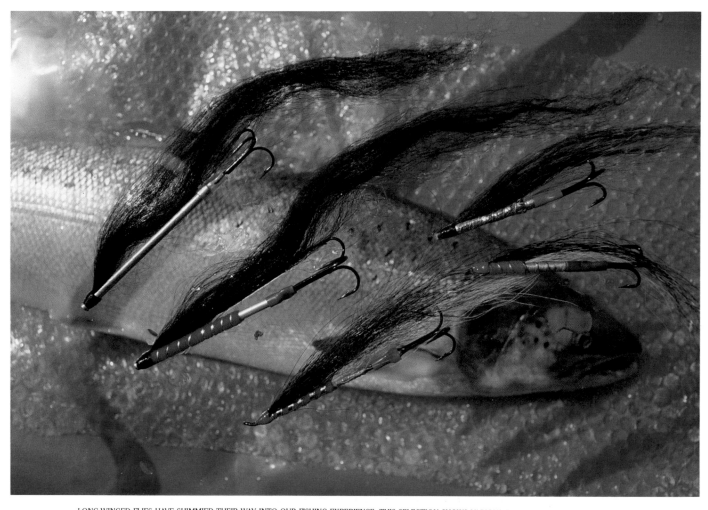

LONG-WINGED FLIES HAVE SHIMMIED THEIR WAY INTO OUR FISHING EXPERIENCE. THIS SELECTION SHOWS VARIOUS PATTERNS. THE LONGEST-WINGED ARE COLLIES. IN ADDITION TO THE SMALL TADPOLE TIED ON A TUBE, THE BLACK, RED AND YELLOW DRESSING IS ALSO SHOWN ON A WADDINGTON.

SALMON TAKEN ON A COLLIE FISHED HIGH AND FAST – BREAKING ALL THE RULES OF EARLY SEASON FISHING WHICH STATE THAT A FLY OF 2–3 INCHES SHOULD BE FISHED DEEP AND SLOW WHILE THE WATER TEMPERATURE IS BELOW 50 DEGREES FARENHEIT.

For once, I was not to be disappointed.

Needless to say, I met my host on a bridge. At least half my fishing trips seem to start with a rendezvous on a bridge. This particular span was at the top of the beat that we were to fish. As old friends, but not having seen each other for some time, we decided to fish down together, taking it in turns to be first down each pool.

My friend suggested that I might like to try a Collie Dog. I replied that he should fish the Collie, while I would try a conventional Black-and-yellow on a 1½-inch tube. We would see who caught what, if anything, because I was still doubtful about the effectiveness of long-winged patterns.

The river was near-perfect in height and colour and that top pool positively reeked of fish. But I fished it down without a touch. There was nothing new in that, of course, but as I was reeling in at the tail, I heard a shout from behind. I turned, and there, halfway down the pool I had just covered, was my friend with a big grin on his face and his rod bowed into a strong-fighting fish.

"One swallow doesn't make a spring,' I told him, but he just laughed. He had opened the scoring, was truly delighted, and tried to tempt me once more with an offer of a Collie, which was steadfastly refused.

By lunchtime, his single swallow had gained two companions. I had only one brief, abortive pull to my credit. Over a mug of soup and a sandwich, it seemed that it was perhaps time to swallow the pill. I asked to look at my friend's fly-box.

Compared to the original Collie that I had seen, his batch – or should I say pack? – were a sophisticated lot. They were tied mainly on copper tubes dressed with red wool, silver Mylar, or a combination of both, with the general appearance of a Peter Ross trout-fly. The tubes varied from as little as 1 inch up to 2 inches or more. The 'wings' ranged from a minimum of about 3 inches, on the shortest tubes, up to perhaps 8 inches on the longest.

I could not help but express my doubts about these flies. As my friend was quick to point out, however, and with that smile still on his face, I was hardly in a strong position to dispute the matter. The facts were blatantly obvious. He had caught three lovely springers. I had caught none. I had to agree that I did not occupy the high ground.

He picked out a 2-inch tube with a red body ribbed with oval silver and a 6-inch black hairwing. I knew his blood was up, because he insisted on leaving his rod at the hut so that he could act as gillie.

"Come on then, the salmon fishing expert," he chortled. This comment raised a smile. We were both prone to defining an expert as an 'ex-spurt, or a has-been drip under pressure'!

Would all fishing instruction were so strongly enforced with such immediate results. I had hardly lengthened a decent line when the fly was swept away by a salmon that turned perfectly in the take.

Later in the afternoon, and two pools further down, I had a second fish, again on the Collie. We took a few moments to admire the beautifully matched pair of eight-pounders, but had to agree that our chances of contacting any more fish were quickly spilling away.

All morning we had been fishing a river in perfect ply, with the water falling and clearing steadily. Since before lunch, however, we had been watching ominous, black rain-clouds rolling over the mountains at the head of the glen. Now the river had begun to rise.

The start of a rise often produces brisk sport, particularly after a long period of low water. But we knew that we would have little more than half-an-hour before the salmon went solidly off the take. There wasn't time for my friend to return for his own rod, back at the hut, so I insisted that he should fish mine. Like the good fisherman that he is, he persuaded a grilse to take the Collie as it swam steadily across the cheek of the main stream. Rain-drops began to sputter down on us, and by the time the grilse was in the net, we were caught out in what would have passed for a monsoon. In a whirl of rod, net and swinging fish, we doubled back to the hut, cracked open a bottle, and took our time to savour the Collie's long wing and tally of fish.

I had been deeply impressed with the obvious attractions of the Collie's long, slinky, black wing swimming through the water, and so, obviously, had the salmon. But I am a perverse creature and went on worrying about the position of the hook relative to the 'wing'. I could not reconcile what I had seen in practice with the theories of salmon-fishing that I had been taught since my boyhood. I had been so thoroughly indoctrinated into suspicion of any wing that trailed behind a hook that I decided to experiment.

Perhaps if I had started by trying something similar to Hugh Falkus's Sunk Lure, as originally designed for sea-trout, my finding would have been different. They could certainly have blurred the issue. Instead, I tied up some metal tubes with long, clear plastic extensions so that the treble hook was carried right back to the tip of the wing, perhaps 6 inches behind the head of the fly.

The first time I fished these creations, I had two long pulls, obviously from taking salmon, which came to nothing. Each time I raised the rod into the take, I felt a brief resistance, and then the line went slack.

Then at the third offer I managed hook and land the salmon. By the best legal definition, that salmon had been foul-hooked. The treble was embedded outside the fish's mouth, in the cheek which would have been opposite to me at the moment of the take. It reminded me of salmon hooked in an almost identical fashion on a long Toby spoon.

It seemed to me that these salmon had swept in at the lure from the side and taken it across its length. Perhaps the head of the fly was visible at one side of the salmon's mouth, and a length of the tube and the treble hook at the other. And when the salmon felt the pull as I tightened, it simply let go of the fly.

My mind turned to memories of the many days fishing for reef pollack in Cornwall. Natural sand-eels were the favourite bait, and I remembered that we fished these bait-fish with the hook placed just behind the gills. On a big eel, this might mean eight inches or more of body and tail would be trailing behind the hook. An exactly similar hooking arrangement is used for artificial eels such as the Red Gill and Eddystone. The similarities in the hooking arrangements of the Collie Dog flies and sand-eels, as well as in their appearance, were quite apparent.

I remembered, too, one day when a small pack of blue shark appeared out of nowhere and began to circle our craft. While my companion hastily rigged a shark trace, I kept the sharks interested by feeding them with mackerel. They would swim over the mackerel, opening their sickle-shaped mouths and rolling back their black eyes in the final moments of their approach. Then they chomped down on the bait fish, which disappeared head first, tail first or whatever. All the sharks were feeding in this way – except for one much smaller chap. He would chomp down and swallow the smaller mackerel, but, on two occasions when he was first to a particularly big fish, he always surged in from the side and took the mackerel on the turn, by its head or as near as made no difference.

Was there a lesson to be learned here? Might we not also learn something from fish-eating birds such as kingfishers, gannets and cormorants? All these birds turn their prey so that they can swallow it head first. If they tried to swallow a fish tail first, the scales, fins and gill covers would stick in their throats. Perhaps the salmon, in taking a long winged fly by the head, or certainly across its length, are simply mirroring this type of feeding behaviour.

I no longer have any worries about fishing relatively short-bodied flies with long wings. I regard the tube, often wrapped in bright tinsel, as the target area, and the logical place for the hook to be positioned – every bit as logical, that is, as the method we use when rigging a sand-eel on a hook to catch pollack!

Long-wings not only succeed in hooking salmon, but they do so superbly. They seem to encourage a salmon to turn in the take, just as I have seen shark do. One problem encountered in fishing standard flies on the sinking line is that some fish come up from behind the fly and take in the laziest of fashions, seeming to take a light hold on it with their lips but without turning. Many such takes are missed, or the salmon comes screaming to the surface, obviously 'tipped' in the nose, and is lost.

The Collie (and its kin, which I have not yet mentioned) does seem to stimulate far more positive takes. Perhaps it is because we fish them a little faster than more conventional, articulated flies that the salmon come in from the side, taking fly, leader and line away in a dramatic whirr of the ratchet before the rod is raised into the take.

Collies seem never to show their best until the water temperature is in the 40s. But this doesn't surprise me. Salmon-fishing lore makes only one big ruling in regard to water temperature: that at 50 degrees Fahrenheit, or thereabouts, salmon show a marked change in taking behaviour. With the water below 50 degrees it is said that they are most likely to show an interest in a large fly fished at some depth below the surface. Above that mark, they are more likely to show an interest in a smaller fly fished close to the surface. What this ignores, however, is the change in salmon behaviour that occurs at about 40 degrees. As the water temperature rises from freezing-point, which it may have reached early in the season, no real change in salmon behaviour occurs until the 40-degree mark is passed. Then the fish are suddenly prepared to ascend obstacles that have created what we call temperature pools; to move into streamier water; and, of greatest interest to the fisherman, are far more likely to move to a well-presented fly.

In the 'old days', when sunk-line gear was not as sophisticated as it is now, gillies and experienced fishermen rigidly followed the rule that, with the water temperature below 40 degrees, you should keep with the spinning rod; that with the water temperature between 40 and 50 degrees, you might try the sunk-line fly; and that with the water temperature above 50 degrees, the floating line could prove the best option. Nowadays, with carbon rods, plastic lines of various sinking rates and weights, and the array of articulated flies, we feel we can fish the fly whatever the water temperature, but we should not lose sight of the fact that the 40-degree mark is critical in terms of salmon-taking behaviour.

I favour a fairly small fly of 2-3 inches, including the treble, when the water is below 40 degrees. I might go up a bit bigger in high water, but generally, when the water is carrying some colour, my first response is to change from, say, a Willie Gunn or Spey Royal to a rather garish fly. This would probably be a pattern with a gold Mylar body and a mixed wing of hot-orange and yellow, with just a few strands of black mixed in; or it might be a Garry Dog. In either case, the size does not normally vary very much. The one exception to my self-imposed rule is perhaps that long-winged patterns should be seen as flies to be fished once the water temperature has topped 40 degrees.

One pattern of long-wing, the Tadpole, is claimed to take salmon in virtually all water temperatures. It was devised by Neil Graesser. To be more accurate, Neil Graesser was on the banks of the Oykel, waiting for the river to fall after rain on melting snow had caused a spate, when, to pass the time, the gillie, Peter Campbell, tied up a long-winged fly to Neil Graesser's directions.

This is described in Mr Graesser's book *Advanced Salmon Fishing*, in the chapter titled 'The Birth of a Fly', and the reason he gives for the creation of this new pattern was that he, like myself, had found that Collie Dogs were not successful until the water temperature had risen into the 40s. To be specific, he gave the water temperature of 42 degrees. If this exactitude seems rather pedantic against my vaguer suggestion, remember that it is at precisely 42 degrees that salmon are suddenly prepared to surmount obstacles. The figure seems to make a lot of sense.

The Tadpole has a long, black wing similar to the Collie's. Its body is red, or crimson, on the half nearest the head, which is finished red, and yellow on the rear half. It has an extra tuft of yellow hair at the rear end to form a tail.

It is possible to take salmon on the Tadpole in water below 40 degrees, so it does seem to transcend the range of water temperatures. However, in discussing Collies, I wrote of flies that might have a 6-inch or 7-inch wing on a 1½-inch or 2-inch tube. Indeed, I recall a reference by Bill 'Rogie' Brown of a salmon taken on a Collie with a wing 'a quarter-of-a-yard' long. But the Tadpole, certainly in my own tyings and those of many others, is best described as a semi-long-wing. By that I mean that many fly-dressers would consider a wing of about 4 inches to be adequate on a 2-inch tube, while on some Tadpoles that I have seen, the proportion has been even less. I can't help comparing this style of Tadpole with the Comet, which does such great execution on Tweed and other rivers. The only outstanding difference between the two is that the Tadpole has its wing restricted to half of the tube's circumference, while the Comet's wing is taken right round the tube.

Is it putting the cart before the horse to say that it is only the semi- long-winged Tadpole that works really well when the water temperature remains below 40 degrees, and that it seems that the truly long-winged version does not come into its own until the 40-degree mark has been passed?

Further evidence may be gained from an experience I had when asking a well-known fly-dresser to tie up some long-wings for me which were to be photographed to accompany an article. He provided a Collie with a wing so long that we literally had to curl it round for it to fit in the picture, while the wing on the Tadpole was barely long enough to trail behind the treble hook. When questioned, the dresser explained that this was the style in which most of his customers liked to have these two patterns tied.

I shall consider what happens when the water temperature eventually tops 50 degrees in later chapters. For the present I shall content myself with saying that whatever the traditional lore of salmon-fishing may lay down about fishing small flies close to the surface, long-wings will go on killing fish. Of course, they are not now on the same scale as those we firmly associate with the 40- to 50-degree temperature range, but, in relative terms, a 1-inch tube with a 3-4-inch wing is quite massive. Nevertheless, they can work like demons when the lore states we should be fishing size 6 or 8 flies, both of which are less than an inch long in standard dressings.

What factors should we consider when looking at the success of long-winged flies? Certainly they include the design's profile and weight. The long wing is a slim, tentative and apparently provocative shimmer in the water, and because the fly is light for its overall length, with an exceptional surface-area-to-weight ratio, it swims in a lively and apparently provocative fashion. Beside the hooking arrangement discussed earlier, these factors could not be achieved by simply tying established patterns on 6-inch tubes or Brora-style shanks. But above all, the one undeniable factor that we must consider in looking at long-wings is their outstanding success in terms of catching salmon.

Long-wings have taught me a lot about fishing for salmon. Some may say that my head is full of fishing theories, but I do not think there is much wrong with that. The only reason that I have had to come up with theories of my own is that I have found so many of the alternatives, inherited without question from previous generations, simply not proven in practice! They force us into a stereotyped approach. Of course, a method will prove 'best', or a certain fly 'most successful', if nobody ever thinks to try anything else.

Practice and experience have convinced some of us that, on certain fishing days, a change in the pattern of fly seems to make a difference. I would suggest that a change in the basic design of the fly may have even greater effect. We might not be able to say exactly why this should be so, but it would be little short of dogma to deny that it *is* so. These long-winged flies are far too useful to be dismissed with a shrug of the shoulders just because they seem contrary to established lore. We may never have an explanation as to why the Collie can be so productive, on its day, any more than we shall be able to say why the black, yellow and orange wing of the Willie Gunn has made it a minor legend. What does it matter, so long as experience shows that it is so?

These long wings are not some sort of piscatorial alchemy. They should be regarded only as a useful alternative to be fished in partnership with our traditional articulated flies. I have no doubts at all that the tube-fly or Brora with standard proportions will continue to take most cold-water salmon for myself and most other fishermen. But there will be many occasions when, if we are not prepared to ring the changes and give these long-wings a swim, we may miss out on a great deal of sport.

The man who spins for salmon has his Devon minnows and Toby spoons as his principal lures. Most spinners will regard the 2-inch Devon and the 4-inch Toby as complementary. Fly-fishers should be able to see the standard and long-winged flies in the same light.

The long-wings have raised other questions in relation to established lore. Generations of salmon-fishers have been raised on the dictum that we must fish 'deep-and-slow' so long at the water temperature remains below 50 degrees Fahrenheit. So what are certain fishermen thinking about when, in the very same conditions, they swim a big Collie fast and barely below the surface of a salmon pool?

Remember, the convention of cold-water fishing it to present a fly *deep and slow*. This is a good convention. It suits most places and most times when the water is cold. But the Collie is producing some thought-provoking exceptions to the rule.

Recent experiences with early-season runs on some Highland rivers have shown that salmon can be roused to take a big Collie swimming quite quickly and just below the surface. A fairly square cast and a high rod-point seem to provoke the most positive response. Sometimes the take comes in an eruption of silver flank in the centre of a mighty surface swirl.

What on earth did the angler who first fished the fly in such a manner, and persevered until he found a taking fish, think he was doing? Such presentation breaks all the rules, bar one. Used at the right place and time, the technique has proved itself an efficient catcher of salmon! Thank goodness for salmon-fishing's happy accidents or eccentrics.

Such thoughts take me ahead, to the autumn. Last autumn was not ungenerous to me, and others. I have no complaints, but a host of memories of fish that moved to shallow-swimming flies. If I had to sum up my autumn salmon fishing of recent seasons, I would talk of flies such as the Comet, tied on relatively small Brora shanks, or perhaps 1-inch copper tubes, fished off an intermediate or slow-sinking line to just settle below the surface; of surface boils in the moment before the reel started to speak; and of three, four and more yards of line going away against the lightly set drag of the reel before I raised the rod to 'mak sicca' of the hook-hold.

This again can be viewed as an exception rather than the re-writing of cold-water tactics. But for many years, most fishermen have seen little difference between spring and autumn tackle and technique, just so long as the water has been cold. Emphasis on what works best for the 'fatter' beats of lower Tweed in October and November denies us the experience and conclusions to be drawn from what is happening upriver, on Tweed tributaries, or on Solway rivers come to that. Here we are thinking about autumn salmon in relatively shallow lies. We simply do not need to fish our flies far below the surface in such places to tempt a salmon. In relative terms, a fly fishing 1 ft below the surface of a 3 ft-deep steam, or at 2 ft in a 4 ft stream, or at 4 ft in a 6 ft steam, are all passing at equal distance of a salmon lying on the river-bed. The search to meet the convention of deep-and-slow must not blind us to the realities of the river at our feet.

In the spring, when we find a shallow-swimming Collie takes salmon when the water temperature is up in the 40s rather than down in the 30s, what should we make of it? It is well to remember that, in rising water temperatures, salmon, apart from becoming more active, are also more likely to be encountered in those relatively shallower and faster sections of a pool.

I think also that the length of the Collie Dog is of great significance. We have a long tradition in Britain of trying to raise salmon to flies fished off floating lines during cold-water conditions, as well as the more usual time when the water temperature exceeds 50 degrees Fahrenheit. Arthur Wood enjoyed some success in this respect, but the shallow-swimming fly has been considered generally as a non-starter in cold water. Might we have done better had we used a much larger class of fly? Experience with shallow-swimming Collies is still relatively new. I would not dream even of hinting that their use might replace our traditional deep-and-slow approach with flies of 2-3 inches. But what I will say is that where the conventional approach is not producing fish, I for one will be happy to seek out a stretch of shallower, faster water over which to fish a squarely-presented Collie with a rod held high. Who knows unless he tries?

Before passing on from the long-wings, perhaps I should offer some 'up-to-the-minute' thoughts on their design. I tie them now with both a long wing and a tail. The tail serves to support the weight of the rear end of the tube and treble hook, thus helping to ensure that the fly swims horizontally. Incidentally, because a short length of extension tubing has to be added to the metal tube to hold the eye of the treble hook, it is advisable to tie in a short tag before the tail which, otherwise, would be crushed by the tube.

I am also experimenting with various patterns. One of my favourite long-wings is one I have christened the Golden Orange. Here is the dressing, for anyone rash enough to give it a swim:

The Golden Orange

Tag: Oval gold.
Tail: Long orange hair.
Body: Gold Mylar ribbed with oval gold.
Wing: Long black hair with a few strands of orange underneath.
Design points: Mylar has a bad reputation for being torn up by taking fish. Therefore it should be tied over a floss base liberally anointed with clear varnish. The oval gold rib also serves to increase the useful life of the fly. The wing-length should be about twice that of the tube and treble hook combined. Thus, on a 2-inch tube with a size 4 treble, the wing and tail would extend 6 inches back from the head of the fly. On a 1-inch tube with a size 8 treble, the wing and tail would extend 3 inches back.

COLLIE DOG – A LOGICAL CHOICE

Natural sand-eel rigged for pollack fishing

Collie Dog on Tube

WHEN TO FISH A COLLIE

When: The Collie works best once the water temperature has risen above 40 degrees Fahrenheit. Salmon show a marked change in behaviour once the temperature is above 42 degrees, becoming more active, being prepared to surmount obstacles, and to take a fly that breaks all the rules and traditions of early-season fly-fishing.

How: Collies can be fished in the conventional manner, being cast downstream at an angle of about 45 degrees and fished across the stream off a sinking line. Equally, there are times, particularly on shallower, faster stretches of the river, where the fly can be cast quite square and fished across the pool quickly and just below the surface on a rod held high.

The Tadpole: This pattern works at temperatures below 40 degrees, but as the wing and tail do not usually extend far behind the hook, the pattern is better regarded as a 'semi' long-wing.

THE BOYS SETTLED DOWN TO WATCH THE AUTHOR'S FAILURE. THEY DECIDED THEIR FATHER SHOULD HAVE BROUGHT A SPINNING ROD, BUT HE FELT THERE WAS MORE TO IT THAN THAT.

BRIGHT CONDITIONS BUT COLD WATER ON THE SPEY. RIVERS SUCH AS THIS PROVIDE A SUPREME CHALLENGE TO SALMON FLY FISHERMEN IN TERMS OF THE CASTING RANGE AND DEEP WADING THAT ARE REQUIRED.

CHAPTER FOUR

APRIL

LESSONS TO BE LEARNED

Success and failure; failure and success. Lessons can be learned from both. Some are about making the right tactical decisions. Others are concerned with recognising conditions conducive to the catching of salmon, and then ensuring that we are in the right place and at the right time to make the most of them.

We're told that confession is good for the soul. However, most salmon-fishing writers seem either to disbelieve that or else to consider that their souls are past redemption! You'll know what I mean if you think how often - or, rather, how seldom - you've read a fishing story that ends with the writer confessing to a blank. But surely this is what happens on most days for salmon-fishers?

I am going to break the 'rule' and recount the story of a trip which ended with my catching nothing. And to make it even more of a confessional, I shall admit that during the two days over which the action (or inaction) took place, seven salmon were taken by other rods on the beat and another three the following morning. It is a tale of wrongly-made tactical decisions, and I would rather pretend that it never happened. But it shows, I hope, that we can learn every bit as much from failure as from success.

It all began when we arrived home from holiday late and with my youngest son with his leg in plaster following an accident. We were due on Speyside next day, so we were up early and slotting into the Easter holiday traffic. The road north is normally fast, but not when it is cluttered by sightseers, and not when they start to panic at a wee blow of snow on the Pass of Drumochter.

Despite the blizzard, the sun was shining when we arrived in Grantown at lunchtime, but by now I was feeling like a piece of chewed string. Perhaps, if I had been feeling just a little brighter-eyed and bushy-tailed, my subsequent decisions would have been better, and I would have had a fish or two.

A trip to Grantown would be unthinkable without visiting Mortimer's Tackle Shop. It was here, at the age of seven, that I bought my first fly-rod – or, rather, my father hovered with cheque-book in hand while Captain Tommy Edwards and Mr Mortimer supervised the proceedings. This time it was Grant Mortimer who had asked me up. His assistant, Mike, greeted me as I came through the door.

"Come on, Crawford! They've had three fish off the beat this morning!

Grant confirmed that three salmon had been taken, and that the gillie would see me at the main fishing hut at 2 o'clock. We swopped news before I set off to gather the family, who were buying the makings of a picnic. I paused in the doorway.

"D'you know what they got them on, Grant?."

"Well, perhaps the minnow, were they spinning, Mike?"

Mike confirmed that they were. Oh, well!

The water looked in great order as we drove along the track beside the beat. A few foot on the gauge, perhaps, but clear. I had no doubts whatsoever, and, after the usual greetings, I told the gillie that I intended to fish the fly.

Now Spey gillies really spoil you. I hardly opened the tailgate of the car before he was asking which rod I would be using. A strong downstream wind was blowing, so I opted for the 17-footer. While I donned my waders, he was putting up the big rod and taping its joints.

"Do you have a slow-sinker with you?" he asked. He would have asked that, of course, for I had a floater, an intermediate, a fast-sinker and a very fast-sinker, but not a slow-sinker.

"No, I am afraid not, but there's an intermediate."

The gillie said nothing, but put in on the rod, and threaded the line through the rings.

"Now, do you have some 12 1b nylon for the leader? It was in the right-hand pocket of my fishing bag. I got on with struggling into my jacket, which should have been on *before* my waders.

Then we went on to the rummage-through-the-fly-box routine. I know that if he had been able to find something like a Willie Gunn, with a long trailing wing and tied on a 1 -inch or 1 $\frac{1}{2}$-inch copper or brass tube, then that would have gone onto my leader. Failing that we ended up with a Munro Killer on a size 4 Esmond Drury treble. It was the long wing, trailing behind the hook, that had 'sold' this particular fly.

In middle-Spey terms, the pools I had been allocated were quite short and could be covered fairly quickly. It makes sense to take a minimum of two good, long paces between casts in clear-water conditions, so that any salmon resting in the pool does not get too much advance warning of the appearance of the fly. I fished up and down these pools until early evening, when we headed back for Grantown. Elsewhere on the beat one more salmon had been taken. As everybody else was spinning, that made the score 4-0, against the fly.

Next morning, because I had only this one day to fish, and the gillie wanted me to see as much of the beat as possible, my name was taken out of the rotation. The beat is normally divided between the six rods with a changeover at lunchtime. However, today I was put at a big, long pool about 150 yards below the fishing hut. I stayed with the 17-footer and intermediate line, but replaced the fly with one of my long-winged Copper Orange patterns, tied on a 1-inch copper tube.

"Now you'll need to wade deep, Crawford, and throw as long a line as you can handle. The salmon lie well over toward the far bank," the gillie advised me before he set off to see how the other rods were faring.

I was not wading quite as far out as the gillie would have liked. The reason was simple: the water would have come over my wader tops. A glance back upstream showed the first salmon of the day being played on a spinning rod. Score, 5-0 against the fly.

A big Spey pool takes time to cover, even by a long-striding wader. But I managed to fish this one three times before lunch. Back at the hut, I learned that the score was now 6-0 against the fly.

After lunch I moved to fish two pools at the top of the beat, where a salmon had been taken on spinner the previous morning. Halfway through the afternoon, and still blank, I saw the family approaching in the car, the gillie in their wake. They didn't have to ask. They could see from my face!

"John, just what the hell am I doing wrong?" I asked desperately.

The gillie stared long and hard at the water before speaking. Perhaps he was wondering whether to risk saying, "Everything!". Instead, he asked whether I thought my fly was fishing deep enough.

I asked Carolyn if she would drive back to the hut and fetch my big black reel with the dark-green line out of my bag and a box of tube-flies.

As she left with the gillie, my two sons settled down on the bank beside the boat that was moored on the pool. I looked at Jamie. He looked at me and sighed: "Should have used the spinning rod, Dad!" said he who sees the Toby as the outstanding, if not the only, lure for catching salmon. I bit my lip and smiled.

Twenty minutes later, the long rod was fitted out with a Wet-Cel 2, a 6 ft leader and a 2-inch Willie Gunn tube-fly. I immediately felt that I was getting down to business, and continued to do so for the couple of hours that were left. But I didn't so much as move a fin!

Back at the hut, I learned that the spinners who had moved down the pool that I had fished in the morning had taken a 12½-pounder from the spot the gillie had pointed out, well over toward the other bank. They said it had taken quite a long cast, even with spinning gear. But that did nothing to lift my spirits, nor to alter the score of 7–0!

We said our goodbyes and drove off. As we passed the Cromdale Bridge a small voice piped up from the back seat. "Dad . . . you know it's my birthday next week?" asked our youngest. "Well, d'you think I could have a new spinning reel?"

I resisted the temptation to suggest he might get a plaster on his other leg, to match the one he had already. But the next week he was delighted to find a fixed-spool hurdy-gurdy among his presents. With the innocence of eight years, he told me I could borrow it whenever I wanted!

So what can we make of all that? Would spinning tackle have been a better choice than the fly? In hindsight, the tale shows such a catalogue of errors, missed opportunities and wrong tactical decisions, that it wasn't so much that the spinner won, but that I scored a few own-goals against the fly. Let me explain.

First, circumstances dictated that I arrived on a unfamiliar beat feeling totally knackered. Apart from the fact that tiredness led me to make mistakes, I always feel that it is far better to arrive at a new beat on the non-fishing Sunday and to take time to study the pools and consider how best they might be fished. Silly though it may sound, on occasions you might even resort to playing 'pooh sticks' - throwing in smallsticks at the throat of a pool and watching them down its length to get an idea of the set and pace of the current. Silly? Perhaps, but it means you start with a better idea of what you are trying to achieve.

Having chosen to fish the fly, I then made some grave errors in the exactitudes of tackle. The gillie recommended a slow-sinking line and a 1 ½-inch copper tube. I used an intermediate line and a size 4 Munro Killer on a relatively lightweight Esmond Drury treble. It seems all wrong now. This is exactly the line-and-fly combination that I often use as an alternative to classic floating-line technique. My own Wet-Cel Intermediate settles just below the surface of a fast-running pool, with the fly fishing at either the same level or slightly above – within 4-6 inches of the surface. This might have been the logical choice had the water temperature been about 50 degrees Farenheit. I might even have got away with it with the water in the upper 40s. But the water temperature was actually in the lower 40s and a biting wind was taking the air temperature even lower. It was foolish not to concentrate on fishing the fly down the fish.

The depth at which we fish a fly is the result of a combination of factors. The slower we fish the line across, then the more it will sink. Equally, it is a result of the line-and-fly combination. A light fly on a fast-sinking line may actually fish at the same depth as an extremely heavy fly fished off a floater. The gillie suggested a medium-medium combination of slow-sinker and copper tube. With the lines in my bag, ignoring the floater, the proper choices would have been either for a fast-sinker-and-light-fly combination or the intermediate line with a heavier fly. In fact, I chose neither and fished a slow-slow-sinking combination.

If I could live that day again, I would use a fast-sinker and reduce the weight of my fly from copper to aluminium to plastic tube, if necessary, until it was not hanking the bottom; or, instead of the lighter tubes, I might have settled on that rather bushily-tied, long-winged Munro Killer on a 4 hook. It might well have worked on a fast-sinking line.

The next part of the saga involves explanation, excuse and confession. On the first evening, I had planned to fish right through to dusk. I stopped at the hut, however, for a cup of tea and a bun at about 6 o'clock. And it was then that two of the spinners invited me to fish 'their' pool, just in front of the hut. I thanked them, had a chat with them, then waded in at the head of the pool as they were leaving. Five minutes later, the sun disappeared. Then squalls hustled down the river and it started to snow. It was that sort of wet snow which, with a wind at its back, is sheer misery to be out in.

Five minutes later, our car appeared. Carolyn had come back early to see what I made of the weather. It was only minutes later that I put the rod in the box behind the hut, stripped off my waders, wet cap, wet scarf, wet jacket and wet mittens, and away we went for something to eat.

Twenty minutes later, the sun was shining again. But the combined needs of four empty tummies and tired heads prevailed. They would not have done so if only I had realised that, of the seven fish taken over the two days, five of them were from the pool in front of the hut. And that had been my only chance to cover it.

What of the fish that I had missed in the big pool the following morning? The simple fact was that I could not cover it effectively by wading from the left bank, even with my longest cast. The spinning rod would have given me that little extra casting range. But that does not explain why I did not hop into one of the boats moored on the river, cross to the right bank, and wade down in front of the trees, double-Spey casting as I went. The gillie had told me roughly where a fish would be lying; it was up to me then to ensure that I covered it adequately. As an alternative to wading, I could have taken the boat into the middle of the stream and let myself down a yard and a cast at a time on the anchor rope.

So why didn't I catch a fish late on the Tuesday afternoon, when I had, at last, chosen a line-and-fly combination that seemed best suited to the prevailing conditions? Well, perhaps by then the pool I was covering didn't hold a taking fish.

I have learned my lessons. Can I put it all behind me now? Let me revert to the great tradition of fishing literature and describe a time when I got things right, even if it does mean jumping to May.

An invitation had arrived to fish and instruct on the Mar Estate water of the Aberdeenshire Dee. This beat lies right up toward the top of the river, occupying the opposite bank to the Mar Lodge water from Linn of Dee downstream to Braemar.

Excellent sport had been enjoyed on the middle Dee, in the Aboyne area, at that time, but the fish had become stuck there on falling water. The water temperature, which might be seen second only to water height in affecting fishing prospects, was good. In fact, it was in the lower 50s. It was water height that was the problem. We needed a rise to bring up a stock of fresh fish. Tuesday evening saw rain-clouds massing over the high mountains, corries and passes, and rain began to fall as we went to bed.

I was first out of bed on the Wednesday morning. At 4 am, as I gulped down a cup of scalding coffee to clear the tubes and allow me to stoke up with the first cigarette of the day, a bleary-eyed Hans came into the kitchen. Wolfgang had been invited to fish the Spey for the next two days, so he was enjoying a lie-in, allowing me to fish his rod. A German swear word broke the silence. Outside the cottage window, a stag was trying his damndest to get at the stacked rods.

Having chased away the young staggie, and with mug in hand, I walked across the road and down to the river. The stick I had embedded on the water mark on the previous evening showed that the river had risen about a foot. It had also coloured slightly. I thought about the snow still lingering on the heights where the rain had fallen, and went to the car to dig out a thermometer. The temperature had dropped back 10 degrees into the lower 40s. No problem, I thought, because I had two rods set up. I would take the 15 footer partnered with a Wet-Cel 2, and leave the floater behind.

That left me to choose a fly. Unless you have dipped into the book at this page rather than reading from the start, you will already know that some places and times give me great confidence to fish with long-winged flies, and with patterns with gold or copper and flash of orange about them when fish are running. I tied on the Golden Orange's half-brother. It is, to all intended purposes, one and the same pattern except that the body, instead of being gold Mylar, is copper Lurex. This particular fly was dressed on a 1 $\frac{1}{2}$-inch aluminium tube, and carried a 4-inch wing of black over orange bucktail.

We fished for an hour or two without result. It was a joy, however, just to be on the river, soaking up the sights and sounds of dawn on upper Deeside. The light was ever-changing as the rising sun filtered through the scurrying grey clouds. The air carried that after-rain freshness that cannot be adequately described in words. Slanting sunlight spotlighted pinewoods and heather-clad hillsides. More than a hundred stags, their antlers still in velvet, grazed within 50 yds of where we fished. It would be a few weeks yet before a combination of heat and flies would drive them from the rich riverside pastures up on to the open hill.

Roderick Haig-Brown wrote that men fish because they like it and it makes them think and feel. He said that if it were not for the feel of water about our legs as we set our feet on rocks or sand or gravel, we should fish less often. A river has its own life and beauty, and the creatures it nourishes are alive and beautiful also.

On such a beautiful Dee morning, my thoughts turned to Haig-Brown's statement that, "Perhaps fishing is, for me, only an excuse to be near rivers. If so, I'm glad I thought of it."

I took time out to sit on a rock and think. I thought of those salmon that had been down at Aboyne before they were stirred by the overnight rise in water. The fish would be bursting through streams and cruising through pools; following their time-honoured running routes. I idly wondered whether fishermen were out and about at Invercauld and Balmoral, and who they might be. It was, hopefully, just a matter of time before the vanguard of new stock passed upstream of Braemar.

Above Braemar, the salmon have an easy passage up sluggish water with ill-defined pools. Typically fast Highland river pools do not reappear until you are up almost to the bridge into Mar Lodge. Then comes a series of rugged pools on the way up to the Linns for which salmon need high water to ascend. That day there was enough water to bring salmon up to the beat, but the Linns would remain impassable. Salmon seem to sense an obstacle in their path, and start to slow down, and perhaps even stop, some distance below. That was why we were happy to concentrate on the pools above and below the suspension bridge.

I looked at my watch. It was just after 8 o'clock, and I was beginning to think that I might have made a mistake in my calculations. I said to Hans that I had been hoping we would have had a fish by now. He simply shrugged. He was still pretending that he couldn't understand English, and I was too embarrassed to try my schoolboy German.

A wisp of smoke curled from the cottage chimney. Wolfgang was up and about. Thoughts of hot, strong coffee, smoked sausage and ham, heavy bread – a solid-style German breakfast. It could wait just a little longer.

I waded in at the top of the Suspension Pool and started to cast. A silvery salmon jumped in the unmistakably purposeful way of a runner, right back in the rough water at the tail of the pool. And then another, and another. I was concentrating hard on fishing the long, slinky fly as slowly and deeply as possible across the central rush of the pool, before accelerating it up through the cheek of the stream. The fly hovered over slabs of rock I had noted when the water was low and clear and where I hoped a running fish might pause for however brief a time. The take came in a long sweep that pulled three, four, then five yards of line away against the lightly-set drag of the reel before the rod was raised to set the hook.

I do not often describe the fight after a salmon has been hooked, but this particular fish, after a strong, cross-river run, allowed itself to be drawn back to my side of the river, and then cruised up the edge of the fast water. A swimming salmon is a wonderful sight. I watched and marvelled as she accelerated strongly toward the neck of the pool. Soon after that, I beached her on the pebbly shore.

Success and failure; failure and success. Lessons can be learned from both. Some are about making the right tactical decisions. Others are concerned with recognising conditions conducive to the catching of salmon, and then ensuring that we are in the right place and at the right time to make the most of them. Salmon are under no obligation to fit in with our social niceties. We must take them on their own terms. That, surely, is the greatest lesson to be learned in the pursuit of salmon.

In a list of required conditions for the catching of salmon, the first and most basic must surely be that salmon are not only in the river, but in the beat or stretch of water being fished. No one can expect to catch a springer in a river where an early-season run simply does not exist, but that doesn't seem to stop fisherman from trying. Equally, the Dee fish showed that rather more than that is involved on my Spey visit, although I did fail dismally in my attempts to make the most of the situation. The fact was that, until the start of the week when I was fishing, only one or two salmon had come off the beat, although it had been fished hard. Then came three in a morning, one in the afternoon, two next morning, one in the afternoon, and three the morning after I had left; and the gillie was confident that catches would continue to rise steadily toward the peak of the Spey runs.

Mention of the peaks of the runs raises a question that may gladden the day-dreams of any keen fisherman who yearns to see salmon stocks returning to their full potential. Is it possible to have too many salmon in the stretch that you are fishing? The answer, perhaps, is a guarded "Yes"!

Having said that, I must explain that what I really mean is that at times a pool may be carrying just too many fish to make it likely that you'll find a possible taker. Fishermen learn to differentiate the jumping habits of salmon. They recognise the world of difference that lies between the slow, surface roll of a potential taker, that may barely break the surface, and the splashy leap of an angry resident.

Sitting on the bank of a Highland river pool that I had covered with a succession of flies over leaping, crashing residents, I suddenly noticed a subtle change in their antics. Their jumping seemed suddenly to have more purpose. Then one fish showed its back in a surface roll. I practically ran down to the river, lengthened line, covered the fish, and 10 minutes later had it safely in the net. At lunchtime, another fisherman asked if I had taken the fish at about 11 o'clock, because he had noted a tiny rise in the water at that time. I had, isn't it nice to have explanations for the difference between success and failure! I had noticed a change in the salmon's behaviour. My companion noted a small rise in water height and had a fish at 11.15am. Each observation had resulted in our flies being quickly in the water and taking a fish.

The often spectacular but apparently purposeless jumping of resident fish seems to suggest that they may be leaping out of frustration. With too many fish for the number of adequate resting places in the pool, a bit of a stramash is going on as to who will lie where. Such sights were more common in the fish rich '60s, but now that stocks are seeming to recover, the sight of large numbers of leaping residents are again not too uncommon.

An elderly gillie once told me that we catch the salmon we don't see. This is not *always* true, but I know what he meant. A pool is fairly hotching with leaping salmon, from its head to its tail, and you feel you simply cannot miss. On a popular public water, a dozen or more fishermen may be thinking the same. A queue starts, but 100 flies and 10,000 casts later, not a fin has been moved. Holiday fishermen will raise their blood pressure and lash the water into a foam. They would fare far better if they waited until dusk and either fished right up in the fast neck of the pool or searched the area above the main holding pool for any spot that might hold a running salmon for a few moments. Alternatively, they could try the tail of the next pool upstream.

My makeshift rule for salmon that show is that if they come up like a nymphing trout, or one sipping down a surface fly, they are well worth a cast. If they show in the porpoise leap that denotes a runner, look quickly upstream for the spot where they might pause. But if they are leaping high and clear, and generally crashing about, then you can virtually ignore them except for the fact that they may be revealing a holding lie that may be worth covering after the next spate, when a fresh stock of fish has taken up their tenancies.

Water-height is the most crucial factor affecting the presence of fish and, most significantly, the likelihood of them falling for our offerings. For example, in a drought season, salmon are either held back in the estuary or become stale, potted and virtually uncatchable in the ever-shrinking pools.

BELOW THE LINNS OF DEE, WHICH ACT AS A BARRIER TO SALMON MOVEMENT WHEN WATER LEVELS FALL. WHEN FISH ARE RUNNING, A KNOWLEDGE OF THE RIVER SHOULD SEE THE FISHERMAN IN THE RIGHT PLACE AT THE RIGHT TIME TO INTERCEPT THEM.

FISHING CONDITIONS – WHAT TO LOOK FOR;

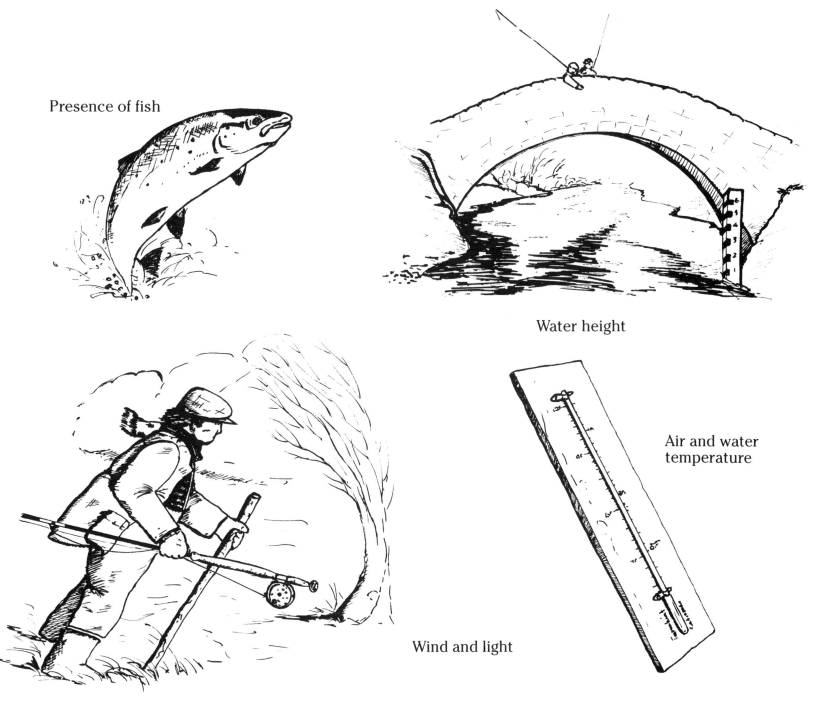

Presence of fish

Water height

Air and water
temperature

Wind and light

On the other hand, we can have too much water. I am not thinking of the raging spate that, on lowland rivers at least, runs the colour of potter's clay for days (which spells disaster, with few exceptions, for all but the worming brigade), but those times when spate follows spate in rapid succession. The river starts to fall, hopes rise of catching fish on the morrow, and then more rain falls and up it goes again.

Smaller spate streams can go up and down like a yo-yo. I remember one October when we lived on the banks of such a river. Conditions looked set for tremendous sport in the closing weeks of the season. A big spate was falling and clearing, with salmon in the river. Tackle was made ready and appointments cancelled. Then came a succession of dry days and wet nights. Up and down, up and down went the level, and the fish just never settled into a taking mood.

Conditions are best when a river maintains a steady, fishing height. This is a rarity indeed on spate streams in the west, but it can be experienced on the classic rivers of the east coast. Spey and Dee are outstanding examples when melting snow runs off through April and May at just the right rate to maintain excellent fishing over an extended period. However, the intervention of heavy rain has its own effect, as well as hastening the snowmelt, and it can be some time before the pools are back at the right height.

Then there is the matter of water temperature. Its main effect is on the taking behaviour of fish. At low water temperatures, certainly below 40 degrees Fahrenheit, salmon tend to be rather sluggish, particularly in the early months. In the later months a drop in water temperature can actually improve the fishing. At the other end of the scale, in high summer, when water temperature soars as the level drops, oxygen is driven out of the water and, in pools with heavy concentrations of salmon, fish can literally suffocate. Such an occurrence was reported on the Thurso, when an enormous run of salmon came in from the estuary on a minimal rise in water. The fish were then trapped in the lower pools and, in the falling water, rising temperature, and reduced oxygen content, they died in their hundreds. We must not be surprised that salmon become comatose when the water temperature is high.

Between the two extremes, sunk-line fishing takes a definite upturn once the water temperature is into the 40s, with, as I have said already, 42 degrees being the critical point at which fish are suddenly prepared to ascend obstacles, to enter faster-moving streams, and to show more interest in a well presented fly. At 50 degrees, or thereabouts, comes the point at which salmon generally are likely to shift their interest from large flies, fished down to them, to smaller flies swimming just below the surface. As a general rule, this is not a bad one to follow, but it should nor be adhered to too rigidly. If a smaller fly is not meeting with success, nothing is lost by giving the deep, long fly a swim.

Most of the gillies I know are quite concerned with water temperature. A Spey gillie will probably say that he likes to see the water temperature rising steadily from the mid-40s to the mid 50s, but a Tweedsider would have a somewhat different view, as he would be concerned primarily with back-end sport through to the end of November.

Opinions also differ on the matter of wind, or its lack. A Spey or Dee gillie will assert that the best wind is no wind at all. One reason for this view is that anything other than a gentle upstream breeze plays havoc with the single-Spey cast, to which most gillies and fishermen on these classic rivers are devoted. But gillies and experienced fishermen on some of the slower, almost canal-like stretches of salmon river in Caithness, the Western Highlands, Hebrides or West of Ireland, will delight in a wind that ruffles slow or steadily flowing water.

My own preference is for a good, stiff blow to put a wave on the water and hide my antics.

Then I feel confident enough for a serious session of backing-up or hand-lining to swim the fly effectively. The only point about which all fishermen are likely to agree is their dislike for a brutal, squally wind blowing straight into their faces. Even exceptional skill in fly-casting cannot make up for the fact that salmon seldom take well during squalls that would have a sailor forever looking over his shoulder.

Next in our search for perfect conditions comes the question of light. It is something that we have to take as we find it. But I always try to avoid fishing a pool which has the sun shining directly downstream. Certainly, few experienced salmon-fishers like a clear, blue sky. Such a light moves my thoughts to fishing at dusk. And a strong or low light sets me worrying about the shadow thrown by a floating line, of which more later.

What is the purpose of considering lessons learned about conditions? Surely the best advice is that it is the fly in the water that catches a fish? Isn't consideration of what we term perfect conditions nothing more than a search for excuses for when we fail to catch fish?

Such questions suggest a rather fatalistic, negative approach to salmon-fishing. If we can learn not only about tackle and technique, but also about salmon behaviour, then we are less likely to waste time, or to find ourselves in the wrong place at the wrong time.

Twenty years ago, I was prepared to fall asleep while wading in a strong stream at the end of a dawn-to-dusk assault on a river. In another 20, I may be prepared to cast a line only in what I believe to be ideal conditions. At present I believe I achieve a balance between the two extremes. The story related at the beginning of this chapter shows what a nonsense I make of my fishing when, due to circumstance, I have to take it at the gallop. I no longer survive six successive days of non-stop dawn-to-dusk activity! And I certainly would not want to do so if the conditions were atrocious, with, say, a high, coloured water, with air and water temperatures all wrong. I prefer to keep ticking along, building up a data-bank of information on the water I am fishing, and then, when the fish are in and conditions are near perfect as any salmon fisherman could reasonably hope, I should have sufficient reserves of energy and concentration to ensure that nothing and nobody drags me away!

SINGLE TURLE KNOT (for use with eyed hooks)

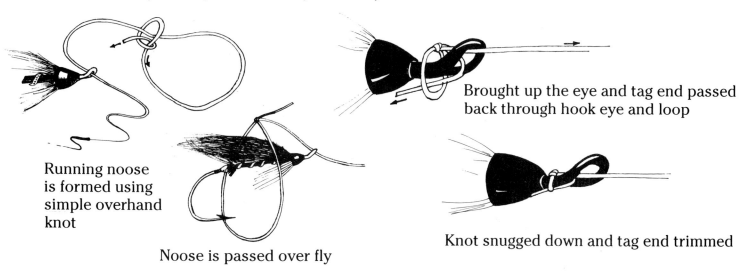

Running noose is formed using simple overhand knot

Noose is passed over fly

Brought up the eye and tag end passed back through hook eye and loop

Knot snugged down and tag end trimmed

BOATS ARE PROVIDED ON MANY SPEY BEATS BUT THE FISHERMAN NORMALLY RELIES ON WADING DEEP AND CASTING A LONG LINE. HE MUST ALSO THINK HARD ABOUT THE DEPTH AND WAY IN WHICH HIS FLY IS SWIMMING.

CLASSIC FLOATING LINE CONDITIONS ON THE UPPER DEE. THE SUCCESSFUL USE OF THE FLOATING LINE DEPENDS HEAVILY ON WATER HEIGHT AND TEMPERATURE, AS WELL AS WIND AND LIGHT ON THE WATER.

CHAPTER FIVE

May

ON CLASSIC FLY WATER

Fly fishing on the Spey or any large salmon river, whatever the season, is heavily dependent upon the fisherman's ability to cast and control a long length of line, and to be prepared to wade deep whenever necessary. The late Major John Ashley-Cooper was perhaps the finest, most effective and certainly one of the most experienced salmon-fishers of modern times. He had the ability to cast, control and catch on a great length of line, and was a confident and capable wader. Such things were what made him a fishing legend in his own lifetime.

Spey, Dee, Tay and Tweed are widely accepted as the four finest salmon rivers in Scotland, Scots would argue strongly that they are the finest salmon rivers in the world. But leaving aspects of national pride aside, if we are talking of May, and thinking about classic fly-water, we can cut the list down to just two rivers: Spey and Aberdeenshire Dee.

A water temperature rising through the upper 40s Fahrenheit and into the 50s gives the nod to waiting fishermen that they may lay aside their most powerful rods and sinking lines. for now is the accepted time for the floating line and small fly fished relatively close to the surface in a style which may be regarded as classic Spey technique, with tackle balanced from the fly back to the rod and reel.

The relatively light flies associated with the floating-line technique are seldom fished off a leader of greater breaking strain than 12 lb, certainly not by Spey casters, and they are not so bulky that they cannot be thrown by an AFTM 9 or 10 line. Now, as we start to think in terms of finesse and delicacy in our presentation of the fly, an AFTM 11 line seems just a little too heavy. My own choice of rod remains a 15-footer, for the Spey demands extremes of casting range, but I look to one with a softer, more through-action. Some folk drop to a shorter rod of softer action, and I do so, too, at times, but when Spey spring salmon, rather than summer fish and grilse, are involved, I keep with my longer alternative.

From mid-May until well into June, the fly-sizes most likely to be needed are 6 and 4, although I do like to have a few of 8 in reserve, just in case the water temperature creeps up faster than expected, or the level falls away. As to patterns, I can hardly believe that any fly kills more salmon on the Spey than does the Munro Killer. With its wing extending back beyond the bend of the hook, and its attractive mixture of black, yellow and orange, with a dash of blue guinea-fowl at the throat, and a turn of gold tinsel on the body, it has the reputation of being the deadliest of modern flies. Add an Arndilly Fancy or two, a Tosh or a Black Maria, and perhaps a Bourrach to my box, and I am happy to fish the Spey with little more.

Fly-fishing on the Spey or any other large salmon river, whatever the season, is heavily dependent upon the fisherman's ability to cast and control a long length of line, and to be prepared to wade deep whenever necessary. The name of the late Major John Ashley-Cooper is inextricably linked with Spey fishing, and he was perhaps the finest most effective, and certainly one of the most experienced salmon-fishers of modern times. Perhaps what made him stand head-and-shoulders above the common run of fishermen was not so much the infinite attention he would pay to his tackle from the point of his hook and through each succeeding link in the chain, nor his confidence in what he was doing and his knowledge of exactly what he was trying to achieve that came only with long experience and thousands of salmon caught, but his sheer ability to cast and control, and to catch on, a great length of line. He was a confident and capable wader. Such things, seemingly so simple, yet so difficult to achieve, were what made him a fishing legend in his own lifetime. It was not so much that he was able to go out and catch a salmon when others failed that set him apart, but that when others were catching twos and threes, he would be catching fives and sixes.

Having chosen rod, reel, line and leader, and tied on, say, a size 6 Munro Killer, much of the rest of your success, within the limitations of your own ability to wade deep and to throw and control a long line, will depend on your own knowledge of where salmon tend to lie at a given water-height in the various pools, on your gillie's advice, or on your own ability to 'read' a river, or perhaps a combination of all three.

Having chosen a small fly, and accepting that, others things being equal, it should swim across the river on its tethered arc as naturally as possible, it pays, on a fast-moving water such as the Spey, to concentrate on fishing the fly as slowly as possible. This is achieved by resisting the temptation to cast too squarely, and by making use of the technique of mending line. Spey pools tend to be scattered with good resting lies for salmon, and it is as well to fish down them quite quickly.

My own method is to move down a minimum of two good paces between casts, and to concentrate on swimming my fly steadily across the dangle by leading it slightly with the rod-tip held high. And I always make sure steadily to draw in a few yards of line, to give a hesitant fish which may have followed the fly one last inducement before I take my two steps down and make the next cast. Covering a pool quite quickly gives plenty of time to fish it down again, perhaps two or three times. Never be afraid to do this. It may seem to be hammering the water, but it is surprising how often a salmon will take on a second or third presentation of the fly. Indeed, my own experience has often been that a fish is more likely to take on the second or third pass than on the first. So I am not always as selfless as I may seem when I step back and say, "You first, sir!" – just so long as I am aware of the other fisherman's ability and willingness to stride on between casts.

With the need to wade deep on the Spey a stout and suitably weighted wading-staff is essential. And local knowledge helps, too. It may not be all that decisive in whether or not you catch salmon, but it could help the total by ensuring that you concentrate on the best places at the right time. For example, you may be well advised to try the necks and tails of certain pools during the fading light of dusk.

What else is involved? Dare I mention a healthy bank balance, which, at the end of the day, can hardly be considered as being of small importance in ensuring you find a salmon attached to your fly.

Does much remain to be added in terms of fishing the Aberdeenshire Dee? Well, not really. Other than normally accepted fly-sizes being a touch smaller than those used on Spey, with alternative, favoured local patterns, few if any differences are noticeable – except perhaps that the Dee does not create the same need for long casting and deep wading as does the Spey, being a little narrower at least in its upper and middle reaches.

The classic, floating-line technique is already well documented, so let me, instead of giving further detailed description, look at its characteristics and what can be achieved with it.

When I was a boy, few people ever questioned whether any alternative method would catch more salmon, at least not in warm-water conditions. It was the late Captain Tommy Edwards who gave the formal finish to the informal casting lessons I had from my father, and he was said to have caught more than 300 salmon in less than a month on the floating line on the Spey, so, make no mistake, I was raised in a floating-line environment! The tackle and technique used have given me great sport over the years, and still do so. But I have slowly realised that, like some fine wines, they do not necessarily travel well, and a knowledge of nothing more than the classic floating-line technique does not stand you in good stead on spate rivers. It has its good days and its bad days even on the classic waters. That is true of all techniques, of course, but more and more I compare the floating-line method with the little girl who "When she was good was very, very good; but when she was bad she was horrid".

That is perhaps taking things a little too far. It might be fairer to suggest that on some days the floating-line technique can be outstanding; but that on others it struggles, and alternatives can outshine it.

In trying to predict when the floating line is most likely to the best choice, we must look for fishing conditions that are as close to perfect as we can hope to find. I went some way to detailing these ideal conditions in the last chapter, but let me summarise:

- The river holds an ample stock of salmon, but not so many that regular disturbance is seen with salmon leaping haphazardly.
- The water has cleared and the level has fallen to, or is holding at, a good fishing height, which will vary from pool to pool.
- The water temperature is rising steadily from the upper 40s Fahr to the middle or higher 50s. (Once the water temperature has risen above that point, would rather see it falling steadily. What certainly does not help is for the temperature to rise one day and fall the next, which seems to upset the fish in much the same way as does an unsteady water level.)
- The air temperature is greater than the water temperature.
- The wind is light and steady. (Gillies say, and most fishermen agree, that the best wind of all is no wind at all. Certainly, a fitful, squally wind is seldom conducive to good fishing.)
- The sky has at least 50 per cent cloud cover. (Some fishermen decry the part played by light, but I fish facing the light whenever possible.)

These are the six factors that I take into account when considering whether the floating line is likely to be successful. They do not all have to be 'spot-on'. Indeed, I can think of several occasions when they have been far from right, and the floating line has still caught fish: days when nobody thought any fish were in the beat, or dozens of them were leaping furiously, or the water was at drought level with a temperature rising in the 60s with the air temperature only in the 50s, or a glaring sun was shining over my shoulder while a gusty wind blew squalls down the surface of the pool, and still salmon were caught! But for now, I will keep to *general trends*.

If you accept those six conditions, what should you do if, say, two or more of them are not satisfied? My view is that if most of them are met, then the floating line should at least be given a chance to prove itself. If *all* of them are met, and no fish are caught, persevere and try to establish where it is that *you* are going wrong. But if *none* of the conditions is met, then an alternative technique is probably the answer.

Salmon-fishing calls for some commonsense. I am at times amazed to see fishermen keeping rigidly to the floating-line technique throughout a long week in which they move not a fin. If the floating line is not producing, and factors in the prevailing conditions suggest why this may be so, then something else should be tried. Perhaps the ease of casting and handling a floating line blinds fishermen to other possibilities. But if the object is to catch fish rather than simply take pleasure from casting a long, straight line, then the salmon must be approached on their own terms. If a particular fly or technique is producing nothing, then surely it makes sense to spend at least some time offering other items?

A successful alternative is at times found through a radical change in tackle and technique. Salmon have been moved to Collie Dogs with 9-inch 'wings', fished across fast steams when the 'rules' have indicated a size 8 fly. Equally, faced with dour salmon, some fishermen have resorted to sinking lines with 2-inch tube-flies and taken fish after fish. It has been suggested that the reason salmon change their attention from large flies fished deep to small flies fished shallow, is that this reflects their feeding experience at sea. They have fed there in cold water on fish of 2–4 inches, but on smaller fish or crustaceans when they have swam into warm ocean currents. This theory seems to me to ignore the existence of the food-chain. Where plankton, crustaceans and tiny fish exist, slightly larger fish will be preying on them, while they, in turn, will be preyed on by still larger fish, I find it hard to believe that a salmon would pass up small herring to snap up a tiny shrimp. It would surely take both.

To my mind, it seems that in cold water, salmon may have fed almost exclusively on vast shoals of immature herring or similar fish a few inches in length, so I am not surprised that, while on the water temperature is above 50 degrees, they have a fairly firm fixation on this size of lure. When the water temperature is above 50 degrees, while smaller prey may create the 'soup' of their feeding, they may not be averse to taking rather larger tit-bits.

Consider some of the Munro Killers and their relatives nowadays considered perfectly acceptable for use with the floating line. Look in a Speysider's box and you may find a Munro Killer tied on a size 6 or perhaps a 4 hook. The wing may be twice as long as the body. So here is, to all intents and purposes, a 2-inch fly. To change from a size 8 to a 2-inch fly or Collie fished off a sinking line may be seen as a radical but sometimes productive departure from established warm-water technique. Another alternative that is as subtle as the other is radical is the use of an intermediate line instead of a floater, one that settles just into the surface.

I have been labelled by some as an idiot who uses an intermediate when others are using floaters. But of course, like all madmen, I am convinced that I am utterly right! But since I first wrote about what I see as advantages in the use of an intermediate, some experienced and well-known salmon-fishers have told me that they, too, now have doubts about the floating line, certainly outside times of optimum conditions, and that they also have been experimenting with the intermediate.

The use of this or a similar type of line for warm-water salmon-fishing is not new. Think back to the early years of the century, and consider the tackle and techniques used by Alexander Grant, designer of the Grant Vibration rods. I have described him elsewhere as a 'no-nonsense' Highlander who corresponded with Albert Einstein and revelled in matters such as the fourth dimension, dynamics and mathematics. Today, he is largely forgotten in fishing circles, but in his time he was something of a legend on Highland rivers, and in particular on Spey and Ness. Indeed, he was affectionately called 'the Wizard of the Ness'.

When Grant put his keen mind to the problems of warm-water fishing for salmon, he decided firmly against the floating line. His methods are described in Jock Scott's book, *Fine and Far Off*. Indeed, it was 'fine and far off' that Grant chose to fish to ensure that a salmon was aware of nothing but the swimming fly.

Grant accepted, as we all must, that thousands of salmon had and would be taken on floating lines, but argued that this did nothing to denyt the fact that the method might be putting down others. He believed that "no fish would like to see a big, black snake floating over his head – and the line would look dark to a fish looking up at it against the light."

The fact is that, particularly in conditions of strong, low light, or when the sun rides high in a clear blue sky, a floating line *does* throw a shadow on to the river-bed. I have seen salmon easing away, ahead of the approaching line and its shadow, as I have watched from a high vantage point while another fished far below me.

It certainly seems that strong arguments can be made against the use of our modern, bulky floating lines in conditions of bright light.

But the argument goes farther than that. Most of us accept that salmon lie higher in shallower, rather faster water than in a deeper, slower stream, and are prepared to 'lift' to take a fly, when the water is warmer. With one or two exceptions, a relatively small fly that is fished quite close to the surface in such conditions is the one most likely to prove effective. No real argument seems to exist about the depth at which the fly should be fishing. The argument is only about the best technique and tackle to use to *achieve* that depth. Should we use a comparatively heavy fly fished below a floater, or a lighter fly fished above a sunk line? My own vote is often with the light fly off a sunk line, because it can be fished slowly but will dart, hover and generally react to the tiniest vagaries of the steam, giving it 'life' even in quite slack water.

The mention of slack water leads me toward another point. It would be unfair to use the names of contemporary fishermen and writers to support my ideas, but I would refer to books by two of the present generation's 'grand old masters' of the sport. Each includes diagrams pertaining to line choice for fishing the small fly close to the surface. Each illustrates the use of a floating line in sluggish-to-medium currents, and a slow-sinking line in a fast current. One shows the intermediate step of a floating line with a sink-tip for use in a fast current.

Mainly because I am such a devotee of the Spey cast, I seldom if ever fish a sink-tip line. The intermediate line serves me for fishing at the same depth. Where does that leave us? Two of our best-known authorities are clear in stating, in terms of fishing the small, close-to-surface fly, that a floating line is advised in sluggish-to-medium currents and a slow-sinker in a fast current, and I am slipping in the intermediate for fishing medium-to-fast currents. But, as any

FISHING THE RIGHT DEPTH

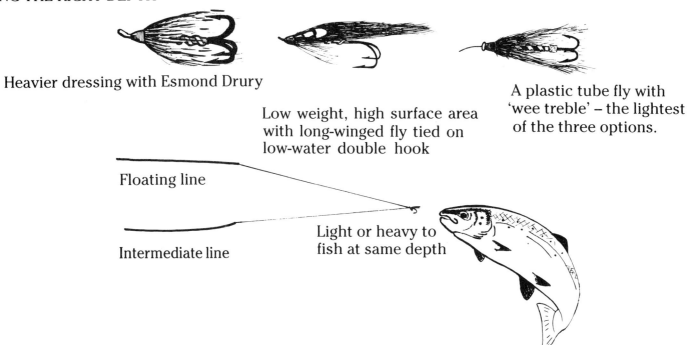

Heavier dressing with Esmond Drury

Low weight, high surface area with long-winged fly tied on low-water double hook

A plastic tube fly with 'wee treble' – the lightest of the three options.

Floating line

Intermediate line

Light or heavy to fish at same depth

Spey or Dee fisherman will assert, it is in the medium-to-fast water that most salmon will be encountered at this time of year. Where does that leave the floater? I don't know!

Let me return to the tackle and technique associated with the intermediate line. First, some questions about the choice of a specific line. I have found, dare I say, that it seems that one maker's intermediate, known also as a 'neutral-density', is another man's slow-sinker. I find the ideal in lines that really are 'neutral-density'. That is, they are virtually the same weight as water, and neither float nor sink. They simply settle into the surface layer of a medium-to-fast moving stream. I can actually watch the Kelly Green of my Wet-Cel Intermediate as it swings across a pool. This gives me great satisfaction and maintains the visual dimension to the sport which we associate with floaters, but which is lacking in a true sinker.

Where intermediates do not match up to floaters is in their ease of handling. Except on a really long rod, such as my own 17-footer, which can raise a great length of line clear of the water on the initial lift into a Spey cast, they have to be cast in the sunk-line style of a roll-cast followed by a Spey if you are to achieve the maximum casting range which is often so essential in terms of covering the water and potential takers. But this is a method concerned with catching salmon, rather than the joys of easy casting!

Equally, little opportunity to mend line occurs except at the moment the line alights on the water. It is, therefore, a method that puts a premium on deep wading and long but necessarily

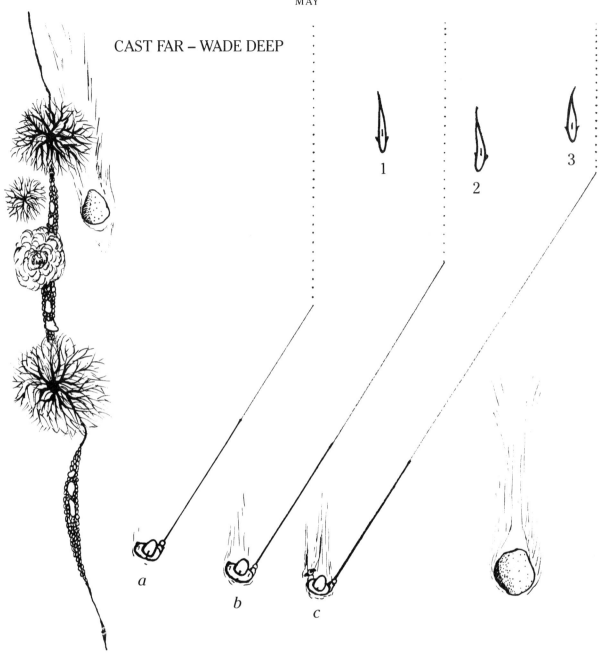

CAST FAR – WADE DEEP

The need to cast and control a long length of line is clearly demonstrated. The short casting, shallow wading Angler *a* fails to cover any fish at all. Angler *b* who wades a little bit deeper and casts a greater length of line covers one fish. Angler *c* however, wades deepest and casts furthest to cover salmon 1, 2 and 3.

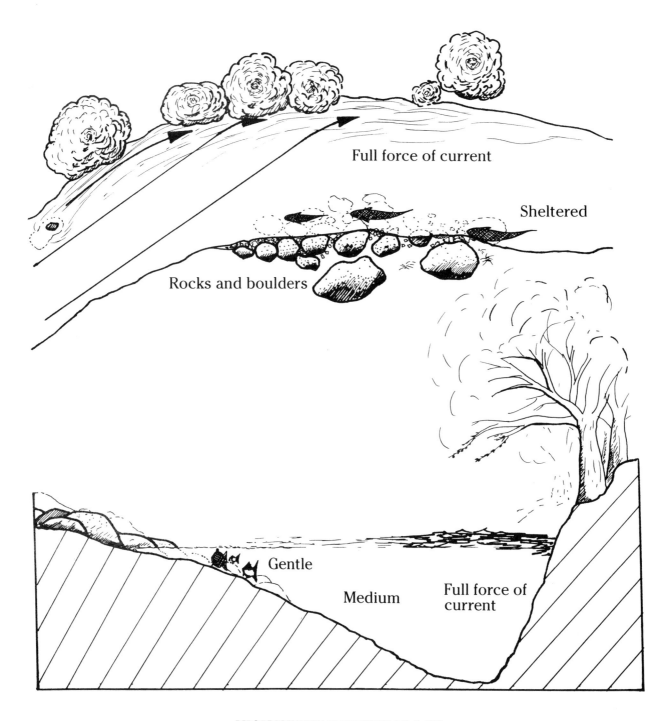

Full force of current

Sheltered

Rocks and boulders

Gentle

Medium

Full force of current

HIGH WATER RESTING PLACE

shallow-angled casts to control the speed of the swing of line and fly. The slower the stream, then the greater the angle at which the cast can be made. Even so, 45 degrees is about the squarest angle at which you would want to cast with this technique, and in really fast streams this might be reduced to as little as 20 degrees from straight downstream – perhaps a little more if a quick mend is made.

I have mentioned a 17 ft rod, but a rod of such length is not really needed. I do use such a weapon on occasions, but a rod which is used for fishing the floating line will deal more than adequately with the intermediate. All that is needed is a spare spool loaded with the new line.

What about the leader? This method, or a similar one, arose from the desire to fish fine and far off. It may be then that a tapered leader and braided butt will help to achieve a sweet turnover of line and a gentle presentation of the fly. Certainly some advantages would come from following this course when flies as small as size 10 or a wee wisp of a plastic tube-fly. With larger flies, I doubt whether a tapered leader would make much difference. I would settle for a length of level line attached to a short length of heavy nylon, needle-knotted to the main line.

My normal practice is to fish 12 lb leaders, with size 4 hooks, 10 lb with size 6, and 8 lb with size 8. This may seem fairly light compared with some other recommendations, but I can with hand on heart, say that I have never been broken by a fish as a result of inadequate nylon. My hand is resting on my desk as I write: I see no point in tempting misfortune.

Anyone who is worried on this point should put up the most powerful fly rod he owns, rig it up for fishing with a 8 lb leader – or even 6 lb – attach a fly, hook it onto a fence wire, and lean back on the rod and try to break the leader. The choice of nylon is best left to individual taste, but having tried most of them, I have settled on Bayer Perlon. Incidentally, my recommendations for leaders are as true for the floating lines as for intermediates. Leader-length should in each case be about 12 ft, including the butt piece.

Standard patterns and designs of fly that we readily associate with the floating line can be used effectively off the intermediate, particularly in fast-flowing water, but the risk is that they may fish a little too deep in modestly-paced streams. It is then, in particular, that it is as well to remember that the objective is a fairly light fly that will fish at or above the level of the line. What is more to the point, rather than weight alone, is the weight to surface-area ratio. Take an Esmond Drury hook and tie on it a standard dressing and wing-length. Now, with an identical hook, tie on a dressing with a longer wing, perhaps twice the length of the hook. The surface area of the pattern has been increased without its weight being altered very much. The long-winged fly, having the greater surface area, will not sink so readily as the standard-winged pattern.

Take this a stage further and dress a fly on a fine-wired low water, double. Now the surface area has been maintained, but the weight has been reduced, so the fly will swim just a little closer to the surface. This ratio is taken to its extreme in the case of a long-winged fly tied on a lightweight plastic tube: a fly that would skate on the surface if fished off a floater.

Out of that can be gained an idea of which flies to choose. I often have a fairly long wing on my warm-water flies; $1\frac{1}{2}$–2 times the length of the hook. If I'm fishing a fast stretch, with an intermediate, I generally opt for a fly tied on an Esmond Drury treble. On a medium-paced stretch, I settle on the low-water double. Slow stretches are few and far between on classic fly-water, but I would probably opt for a wee plastic tube, or the low-water double, which I would accelerate by hand-lining or square casting.

When I first wrote about the intermediate line, I had a suspicion that readers would consider that the whole technique was fuss and nonsense. Even now some may think that it can't make tuppence of difference whether a fly is fished at 6 inches below a floating line, or at the exact same depth but at the same level as, or above, an intermediate. Well, I think it does. The differences may be so subtle as to be verging on the negligible, yet, my goodness, what a difference it sometimes makes in practice! I am now far from being a lone voice in saying that, for which I am thankful. I was starting to feel rather lonely in my private asylum!

IDEAL CONDITIONS FOR THE FLOATING LINE

- There should be an ample stock of salmon in the river, but not so many that you are witnessing signs of regular disturbance with salmon leaping haphazardly.

- The water has cleared and the level has fallen to, or is holding at, a good fishing height. This will vary somewhat from pool to pool.

- At the time of year under discussion, the water temperature is rising steadily from the upper 40s Fahrenheit and on to the middle or higher 50s. Once the water temperature has risen much above that point, it would be better for it to be falling steadily. What certainly does not help is the water temperature to rise one day and fall the next and so on. This seems to upset the fish in much the same way as unsteady water levels.

- Air temperature should be greater than the water temperature.

- A light and steady wind. On classic, floating line water, most gillies would argue, and most fishermen agree, that the best wind of all is no wind at all. Certainly, a fitful, squally wind is seldom conducive to good fishing.

- At least 50 per cent cloud cover. Whenever possible, fish facing into the light. Do remember that a salmon is not blessed with eye-lids.

CHAPTER SIX

June

GRILSE IN THE GLOAMING

Grilse and summer salmon are an attractive proposition, and not only because we seek them out in what is very often shirt-sleeve weather. They are neither the biggest nor hardest fighting of fish. They will seldom outclass a sea trout, pound for pound, but they do give great sport and can quickly sort out the novices from experienced fishermen who know to fish in the right places at the right times, and to vary their tackle and technique until they find a winning combination.

When we lived in the West Highlands, I could work late at the office and, with only 20 minutes drive to the river, still have time to try for a salmon or grilse before turning my attention to sea-trout. One evening, soon after I'd started, the water bulged in a flash of bronze and silver beneath the Black Pennell I was fishing on the dropper. I saw the fish, but felt nothing. A few minutes later, I felt a short, sharp tug and presumed that the fish had been interested in the Silver Stoat tube on the point. But that incident set the pattern for the whole evening. It became a farce of plucks and missed takes, hasty changes of fly, in both pattern and size, and a frenzy of contrasting tactics. You name it, I tried it. I did manage to fool a small grilse that positively threw itself at a small but long-winged reddish fly that I fished fast past a deep, bouldery lie. Perhaps that fish had been born unlucky.

Then, at just the time I thought I should be concentrating more on sea-trout, I had another take from a bonny little grilse; and then a salmon, and finally another grilse, after which the sea-trout stole the show.

On a different day, following a spate on another northern river, two of my friends were fishing a highly productive beat. Conditions seemed as near perfect as possible. They told me later of watching small groups and shoals of grilse cruising in unsettled manner in the pools, and of the sheer frustration of plucks and snatchy, missed takes. Many of the fish with which they had brief contact simply tore off downstream before wriggling about on the surface and freeing themselves. They swear they moved more than 100 fish, but they ended the evening with seven, most of which were grassed late on.

To read reports of these days in terms only of figures, might give the impression that

FISHING STREAMY WATER AT DUSK – A PRIME TIME FOR GRILSE.
A FAIRLY LARGE FLY CAN WORK WELL AT THIS TIME. PERHAPS A 3
INCH WINGED COLLIE DOG DRESSED ON A 1 INCH TUBE AND ARMED
WITH A TREBLE HOOK.

GRILSE FISHING IS OFTEN AT ITS BEST DURING THE FADING LIGHT OF DUSK. THIS IS THE TIME WHEN NATURE STIRS, AND SUMMER
SALMON AND GRILSE MAY CRUISE IN THEIR POOLS.

outstanding sport had been enjoyed. "Mr Little had three grilse, one salmon and a fine basket of sea-trout in one evening." "Mr Smith and Mr Jones had seven grilse in a brief but spectacular burst of activity . . ." What hidden truths such reports can hide! Of course, we had nothing to complain about, but we certainly had plenty to think about.

An inspection of my fishing diaries shows that in bright, hot weather, most of my summer salmon and grilse are taken in the few hours before dusk or after dawn: grilse, then on to sea-trout as the embers of the day die, then back to grilse in the light of early morning. Before and after these times, productive encounters may be very much the exception.

Do we not often experience evenings that start with a succession of snatchy, abortive takes before the sea-trout settle and show a degree of sincerity in moving to our flies? It can be frustrating, but we fish on for the delight of connecting solidly with one of these fine, sporting fish.

On one pool of a certain salmon and sea-trout river that I am lucky enough to fish each season, I have learned to steel myself to the fact that in exactly the same light in which I would be having sincere takes from sea-trout on virtually any other river, the sea-trout produce only a catalogue of abortive pulls and plucks. Then, predictably but suddenly, the rod arches, the reel screams, and the inky-black stillness comes alive to the sloshes and swirls of a fighting fish. Slowly, the reel's screams settle to a song, then an angry chatter, and finally silence – until, that is, the next sea-trout takes. It makes no difference whether large or small flies are used, a floater or sinker, or whether the fish are stale residents or as fresh as paint; nor, for that matter, whether I have seen one or two magpies earlier in the day. This pool simply refuses to show its best until the darkest hours of the night.

We accept that sea-trout are best approached between dusk and dawn. Would we, in anything approaching normal conditions, confine ourselves to fishing for them outside this period? I don't think we would, or should. And so it is perhaps with grilse: we should decide whether or not social and domestic arrangements should be allowed to take precedence over the fishing. Once you accept that to catch fish, you must take them on their own terms, you can start looking forward to rather more success, even if it is at the cost of appearing anti-social.

I remember an evening when I found time for a second cup of coffee after an early-evening meal. The crunch of tyres on gravel announced the arrival of the first party returning from the river. In they came, looking tanned but not particularly happy.

"My goodness, those fish are tight. We saw plenty, but caught only one. Mike had it on a tiny wee Stoat. What will you have, Crawford?" Mouths dropped in amazement as I declined the kind offer.

This party was paying a small fortune for the beat, and as I drove down to the river, I couldn't help smiling at the thought of the sport their gillie would be enjoying after he had finished his tea.

Half-an-hour later, I had a stretch of what is normally considered hard-fished public water to myself. The sun, which had been blazing down on the strath all day, was easing down in the west as I started to cover the strong, wide stream as it spread across the breadth of the pool. I raised the rod-point after a short cast to bring the dropper scuttering back along the surface. A sea-trout of just over 2 lb came in a flash of silver flank and gave a good account of itself.

Some time later, when I had moved further downstream but the flies were still playing

AN EDDYING BACKWATER

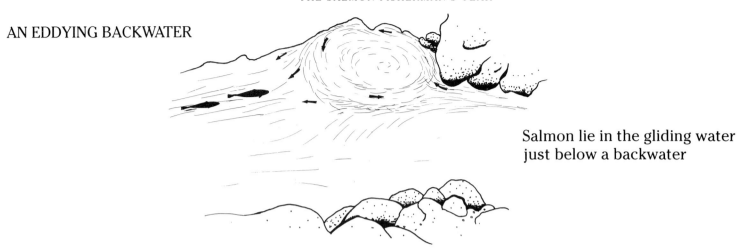

Salmon lie in the gliding water
just below a backwater

across fairly shallow, streamy water, a boil came on the surface as the floating line seemed to jump off the water, and then everything went slack. Next moment, the rod bent into a dashing little grilse, but the hook fell out. I replaced the double with a tiny Waddington, armed with a wicked little outpoint treble. The next fish was firmly hooked, and its capture restored a modicum of decency to my muttered language.

Such fishing for grilse with lightweight tackle is one of my favourite aspects of gamefishing, especially with the added bonus of possible tussles with sea-trout. Both species react well to a sensitive approach.

Grilse are notoriously difficult to hook and hold. Knowing that, it is small wonder that so many experienced grilse-catchers favour a treble-hook. At times a fairly 'dumpy' fly seems best, and then an Esmond Drury is to be preferred. At other times, a rather slimmer-profiled and slightly longer fly seems to have the edge, and that is when a small Waddington or similar wire-shanked fly can work well. Popular patterns are many, but for streamy water I like a fly with a silver body, such as the Bourrach, Silver Stoat or Kenny's Killer.

When I fish a dropper, which I do a lot during the summer months, although I prefer the hooking potential of a treble, it does have an awful tendency to cause tangles, so I normally settle for a strong-wire, wide-gape single with a snecked or reversed bend. A Black Pennell is often my first choice. With soft hackles, and in a strong stream, it must look almost identical to a Stoat's Tail. The Black Brahan with its black hairwing over a red Lurex body ribbed with oval silver tinsel is another useful fly for grilse and sea-trout.

When a floating line is being used to fish a fast stream, a quite heavy but small fly will help to maintain depth. A light fly simply skates on the surface, or 'scratches' it. It is now that the smallest of brass tubes might be chosen, adorned perhaps with a silver body, or no body at all, and a few strands of black hair, and armed with a small treble hook, perhaps size 14, either black or silver. Some fishers swear by a silvered treble in these smaller sizes, but whatever is chosen, it must be the best. Nothing is so annoying as to have a hook straighten or break because it has not been correctly tempered. A hook should not be too soft, but neither should it be brittle.

The smallest of those rule-breaking Collie Dogs and Tadpoles should also be considered. A typical Collie for summer use might be nothing more than a bare 1-inch aluminium tube with a 3-inch black hairwing. If this is too light, a change should be made to a pattern dressed on a copper tube.

That covers a fair range of patterns and sizes of fly but to be a little more specific, and leaving aside the Waddington, Collie Dog and other alternatives, the general rule in summer conditions is to fish a small fly - perhaps a size 8, 10 or smaller Silver Stoat tied on an Esmond Drury hook might be seen as typical.

Size of fly affects the rest of the tackle, if a balanced outfit is the aim. A leader of no more than 8 lb breaking strain might be the choice, and this would suggest a rod and line combination of AFTM 8 or thereabouts. The general rule is that the AFTM number should be no more than one greater than the breaking strain of the nylon. Thus, if in the lowest of water conditions, perhaps with a size 12 fly, a 6 lb leader is chosen, then great care must be exercised if a rod more powerful than AFTM 7 is selected.

All this is leading to the realisation that rods and lines for the pursuit of grilse are perhaps best in the range of AFTM 7-9.

But rather than write vaguely about grilse rods, let me offer examples of some that I regard as logical choices – unless, of course, larger flies are the choice, when double-handed AFTM 9 and 10 rods will suffice.

A few seasons ago, I did virtually all my grilse fishing with a 10 ft 6 in single-handed rod rated AFTM 8-9, or a rod on which the manufacturer suggests either an AFTM 8 double-taper, or a 9 forward-taper should be used. Since then, however, I have drifted back to lighter and longer alternatives. Nowadays, if I decide to fish single-handed, my first choice is normally for my 11 ft rod rated AFTM 6-8. This is an excellent weapon with which to present the smallest flies on light leaders with delicacy and accuracy, while maintaining casting range and water command.

When I do not feel the need to fish quite as fine, I revert to a double-footer handed rod – a 13 rated AFTM 7-10. This Spey-casts superbly with an AFTM 9, but I drop to an AFTM 7 or 8 for overhead casting. Oddly enough, in this age of super-long double-handed rods, this 13-footer fished with an 8 line is just the sort of weapon that most of us used for summer work in the days before carbon-fibre.

Why and when do I choose a double-handed rod? The answer is: 'Most of the time'. Single-handed rods are great fun to fish with, but the longer double-handed rod, gives far more effective line control. To me, and for summer work, this is extremely important. And so, despite the fact that I have caught many salmon on single-handed rods of all lengths, including 9 ft and less, in American style and consider it great sport, when it comes to fishing with maximum efficiency for minimum effort, my vote is for a double-handed rod, albeit of a lighter type.

Such a rod is very sensitive, and, 'telegraphs' the merest twitch of a take. In summer, I fish with the line running over the index finger of my upper hand on the rod, and I have been amazed at the number of occasions I have responded to what has seemed the faintest suggestion of a take and made solid contact. At other times I have inadvertently foul-hooked a fish which has presumably been moving to the dropper. It has seemed almost as if I have sensed, rather than felt, their backs brushing the leader and, in tightening in response, have accidentally drawn the point-fly into their flanks. This is something I would prefer to avoid, and I mention it only as an illustration of the degree of sensitivity inherent in shorter, double-

HAND TAILING A GRILSE – ALWAYS ENSURE THE FISH IS THOROUGHLY BEATEN BEFORE LEADING IT ASHORE. WHERE A SHELVING BEACH IS AVAILABLE, THIS IS THE SIMPLEST AND SAFEST METHOD OF GETTING A FISH TO DRY LAND.

handed, carbon rods.

This begs the question of whether or not I 'strike' grilse. In saying that I do, I would also argue that I tighten rather than strike. What is the point of doing otherwise when fishing with a small treble? Equally, a single with a snecked bend will cork-screw itself into a secure hold, or not, as the case may be. Singles always pose a problem in regard to hooking, but by fishing trebles, and tightening the moment anything is felt, the results are not too bad, even with the notoriously difficult grilse. If you feel a fish at the end of your line, it must have closed its mouth on the fly, so waste no time in twitching home the deadly little hook.

My own view of 'feeding' slack line to a taking fish by holding a yard of line in a loop and letting it go when a fish is felt is that, while I have seen some strong theoretical arguments for it, it does not seem to work as well in practice – at least not for me. However, I do like to keep the rod-point slightly raised while the fly is fishing across, so as to create a little 'droop' in the line. This and the inherent degree of stretch in most modern plastic lines ensures a nice, even tightening, and avoids any suggestion of a snatch at a take.

I do *like* to use a floating line, and normally I persevere with it unless the reaction, or lack of reaction, of the fish demonstrates that it is not creating the right illusion. But the subject cannot be wrapped up in a discussion of line types. What we are really concerned with is a combination of fly (which may be one of a number of designs, all with different swimming characteristics), leader and line. This trinity of tackle is inextricably linked, despite its possible permutations, and has a profound effect on the eventual presentation, and not only in terms of depth.

When I try to decide what is happening when grilse come to the fly with plucks and frustratingly short takes, it seems to me that if I actually see the fish, I tend either to fail to hook it or I have it on for only a few seconds. Am I simply snatching away the fly? No, I don't move quickly enough for that. I steel myself *not* to tighten until I actually *feel* the fish. However, if I am aware of virtually nothing except that a fish is on, the hooking is generally good. I suspect that the small, light flies that we associate with grilse fishing may sometimes be just a little too close to the surface when fished off a floating line.

A number of experienced fishermen, who fished in the 1940s, 1950s, and 1960s, have told me of their feeling that salmon seem far less prepared to show themselves in the take thant they were before the outbreak of UDN (ulcerative dermal necrosis). This may not be simply a case of looking back through rose-coloured glasses, because I, too, remember fish showing well in the take in the mid to late 1960s, although, as a salmon-hungry teenager, I was not really interested in how they took, just as long as they did.

Certainly, fishing books and stories of an earlier generation are filled with summer fish that took sincerely in a head-to-tail surface roll. Nowadays, we seem to find that it is the fish which does not show in the take, other than a hint of a bulge in the surface, which leads to firm contact. It seems to me that North American salmon regularly show as they suck in a wet fly, and they, of course, come also to a dry fly. Despite some success with the dry fly on certain Highland streams, and occasional triumphs with the riffled and dibbled fly, this does not belie the general trend in British salmon-fishing.

Thinking of June, grilse and summer salmon always brings me back to comparisons with sea-trout. Sea-trout hump, bulge and break the steady surface of a pool tail in the dusk when they are fished for with a floating line. On the other hand, many experienced sea-trout fishermen have practically forsaken floating lines in favour of intermediates. They use the line regularly, together with sink-tips, slow-sinkers and fast-sinkers and so on. I read not long ago an experienced sea-trout fisherman who described his sea-trout lines in diminishing order of importance: intermediate, slow-sink, fast-sink and, last, floater, which he said he used only for a minor tactic involving a surface lure. In Scottish terms, this is returning to the tradition of fishing for sea-trout with a silk line.

I do not seek to deny that salmon, grilse and sea-trout will move to flies fished on, or scratching at, the surface. Far from it. Techniques that employ this style of presentation work well at times, particularly on small spate streams. Dibbling a fly on the surface works well n some northern water, and is particularly favoured on the Helmsdale, especially on fast, broken streams in the neck of a pool. But even the late Jim Pilkington, one of dibbling's greatest exponents, did well to hook six out of ten offers, and many would be happy to do half as well. The fact that a few rivers will produce fish to a fly fished in or on the surface must not obscure the more general trends on most other rivers, from which most salmon and grilse are caught. Dare I say that we can all be led astray when fishing writers try to find something new to write about?

The intermediate is one alternative to the floating line, and in fast, streamy water it will hold a fly just those few vital inches deeper than a floater – deep enough to allow a fish to take in a bulge but without breaking the surface. It is also a useful choice in bright weather, when we may worry about a floating line throwing a shadow. Fished over still water, and when being hand-lined, the intermediate also eliminates line wake. And handled properly, it is more pleasant to use and allows more delicate presentation than any commercially-produced sink-tip.

I was for a long time opposed to sink-tips. I bought one about 15 years ago, and eventually threw it into the back of my fishing cupboard. It was no more than a long section of sinking line attached to a floater and, apart from its awful casting characteristics, was too much of a 'twixt and between' to be of use in the pursuit of salmon. I believe that salmon flies should be fished either deep, or within 8 inches of the surface. Sink-tips, it seemed to me, gave a mid-water presentation. This may work at times, but I prefer the more extreme styles, and so, it seems, do the fish. I still have little regard for such lines.

What I do like, however, is what I call an anti-skate line rather than a sink-tip. I make up my own anti-skate lines by using a yard or two of running line off the back section of a worn-out, forward-taper sinker spliced and super-glued to the front of a double-taper floater. This line Spey-casts and mends and fishes well. I use it a lot when the sun is not too bright and the water not too slow or steady.

A modern alternative to this form of anti-skate line is available in the various types of sinking braided leaders, but it is too early to deliver a final verdict on them.

But all this talk about anti-skaes, sink-tips and intermediates should not blind us to the fact that the good old floater still catches most of our summer fish. Outside of bright weather and stillwater conditions, I am delighted to use a floater. However, I do like to use a fairly heavy fly when fishing fast, streamy water, and so avoid having the fly 'scratching' at the surface. It might be a lightly-dressed Esmond Drury, or it could be, in extreme cases, a copper-bodied tube-fly.

Whenever and wherever the floating line can be rationalised as the correct choice, it is far more pleasant to handle than any of the alternatives. It casts superbly, gives a great sense of being in control and in contact with the fly or flies, lifts off the water with the least possible disturbance, can be placed accurately, and, with some mending here and hand-lining or leading there, can be 'hovered' or accelerated virtually at will. In a fast stream, the current will give a small but heavy fly all the semblance of life. In slacker and medium-flowing water, a rather lighter fly may be selected. Always the object is to fish the fly from 4-10 inches below the surface. Then up jumps the floating line in a fine kick of spray and a grilse is on – marvellous stuff!

Do grilse and summer salmon in large river flows make their own rules? Well, they certainly ease the emphasis away from sensitivity and more toward casting range and water command. On rivers such as Spey and Ness, while much fishing may be with single-handed rods and double-handers in the 12 14 ft class, many experienced fishermen will still use a 15-footer except in the lowest of low water, albeit not such a powerful model as they used for sunk-line work in the opening months of the season.

The Tay, mightiest of all Scottish rivers, certainly does write its own rules. The search for extreme casting ranges can become something of a phobia when the far bank seems to merge with the horizon! Many Tay fishermen are loathe to part with their spinning rods at any time of season. Those who do fish fly during summer recognise that their approach is often centred on deep-wading with long casting, demanding enormous upstream mends and a rod pointed straight out across the stream to fish the fly effectively over a mid-river lie.

Do not expect too much sympathy here for the single-handed approach. I have told the tale before of the Tay gillie on his own beat who, when he saw me rigging my 17-footer, came up with the marvellous remark: "That's a grand wee rod," and he was being serious! It turned out that he regularly used an 18-footer and was putting aside something from his tips in order to be able to afford a 20-footer.

Stronger leaders are needed with these longer rods. Here again we see that big rivers, on the whole, tend not to need the smaller class of fly.

I am a fan of grilse and summer salmon, and not only because we seek them in what is often shirt-sleeve weather. They are neither the biggest nor the hardest fighting of fish; they seldom outclass a sea-trout, pound for pound. But they do give great sport and, particularly in rivers that fall outside the 'classic' definition, quickly sort out the more experienced fishermen who fish in the right places at the right times, and vary their tackle and technique until they find a winning combination.

Summer fishing on many rivers, including Spey and Dee, where coastal and estuary nets are no longer operating, is possibly due for a bonanza. The demise of many nets may see the early-season runs returning to their former glories, but I think it will be grilse, summer salmon and summer sportsmen who will benefit in the short term.

SUCCESS WITH GRILSE

Fishing conditions: Summer spates are needed to bring fresh fish into the river and beat. Fishing will be at its best when the river is falling and clearing. After that, the high summer sun should be avoided by concentrating effort on the dawn and dusk periods.

Flies: Grilse and summer salmon can be taken on a variety of fly patterns and sizes. Waddingtons up to 3 inches long can be effective on a falling water, as can the smaller sizes of Collie Dog and other long-winged patterns.

Once the water has fallen a little further, smaller, more conventional flies can be used, tied on Esmond Drury trebles or double hooks in patterns such as the Bourrach, Silver Stoat, Black Stoat, Shrimp Fly, Black Brahan and Hairy Mary. A dropper can be effective – perhaps a Black Pennell tied on a strong wire, wide-gape, snecked-bend single hook.

Leaders: It may be necessary to give salmon the benefit of the doubt at times of low, clear water, and fish fine leaders of 6 lb or 7 lb, in which case a sensitive rod must be used. With size 8 and 10 flies, however, it should not be necessary to go below an 8 lb breaking-strain leader.

A SINGLE-HANDED ROD IN USE ON A WELSH RIVER – BUT THE AUTHOR OFTEN CHOOSES TO STICK WITH THE DOUBLE-HANDER. IT OFFERS JUST THAT LITTLE BIT EXTRA IN TERMS OF CASTING RANGE AND EFFECTIVE LINE CONTROL.

PLAYING A STRONG SUMMER SALMON THAT TOOK A TINY FLY INTENDED FOR GRILSE. IN THESE RIVERS WHERE HEFTY SALMON MIX WITH SUMMER GRILSE, THE FISHERMAN MUST BE CAUTIOUS OF FISHING TOO LIGHT.

CHAPTER SEVEN

July

WHERE WATERS FLOW SLOW

Some stretches, beats and, indeed, entire rivers have little or no flow except in times of spate. Some of the lower reaches of rivers amid the flat, low moorlands of Caithness are almost canal-like, and many so-called spate rivers are characterised by sluggish stretches. What they all have in common is an ability to produce fine summer sport. But they must be approached in the right way.

The thought of a medium-to-large flow of fast water through clearly defined runs, pools and streams is enough to make a dedicated salmon-fisher's eyes glaze over. Individual thoughts of ideal summer water vary from one fisher to the next; one may favour this river, another will favour that; but in nine cases out of ten, perhaps, the essential ingredients remain the same – a lively flow in which a fly can be cast at an angle of about 45 degrees downstream. Apart from the need for an occasional upstream mend, plus a few slow draws at the line before it is lifted for the next cast, a cast can be left to its own devices. The fast-moving current is sufficient to ensure that the fly swims attractively across the stream.

This is not exactly a demanding technique. You may argue, if you favour larger rivers, that it calls for a degree of accomplishment in deep-wading, casting ability and line-control. However, it is, in terms of fishing the fly, a negative rather than positive approach to the catching of salmon. It works well in most places most of the time, and undoubtedly takes most fish throughout the season, but having chosen appropriate tackle and learned how to use it, should we not be concerned with things that we should do rather than with things we need not? I hope you see the distinction.

There are alternatives which make us think and do a whole lot more. Salmon rivers come in all sorts of sizes and types, and as the demand for fishing increases, more and more salmon-fishers find themselves on waters that are far from being in the classic mould. Some are so removed from what we might see as the ideal that they beggar comparison. But make no mistake, those fishermen who are prepared to approach such rivers and their fish on their own terms, have great sport and satisfaction to gain. Indeed, some fishermen find that the thrill of success on such waters is such that they soon forget about classic water and its tackle and techniques.

Rivers are fast, medium-paced or slow, just as fast, medium and slow stretches exist within a river, and all of them can hold salmon. Fast and medium flows respond well to the classic and fairly stereotyped approach. Slow flows demand a different approach altogether.

We were taught, as beginners, that salmon lie in slower, deeper water during the colder months of the season. Then we were told that, as the water warms, salmon move into faster and often shallow water. This is fair enough, in so far as it goes, but it is rather too black and white, without shades of grey. In fact, these statements are best regarded as only half-truths, and therefore apt to mislead. They disallow the fact that a discussion on salmon fishing has little room for words such as 'never' and 'always'.

A summer salmon and grilse fisherman who ignores the possibility of his quarry choosing to rest in slow flows is denying himself the chance of finding fish outwith clearly-defined and recognisable salmon pools. He fails to recognise what he is missing. Most of the advice he has received will not have prepared him to think outside the classic approach to salmon, and so he passes without a second glance any number of spots which may hold a taking fish. We are probably all guilty at times of failing to understand that salmon will choose to lie in what we see as highly unlikely places.

Some stretches of water – beats and, indeed, entire rivers – have little or no flow except in times of spate, yet they hold large numbers of summer fish. Some of the lower reaches of the Thurso and Wick river amid the flat, low moorlands of Caithness are almost canal-like, and many so-called spate streams of the West Highlands and Hebrides are characterised by sluggish stretches between still lochans. You would be hard put on some to point to the spot, let alone the area, where a loch ends and a river begins. Ireland has tremendously productive but slow-moving rivers such as the Erriff. What they all have in common is an ability to produce fine summer sport. But they must be approached in the right way.

Even rivers in the traditional mould have slow-flow areas. A river without them is rare indeed. They are to be found even on rivers with reputations for being among the fastest-flowing. I have sat on the banks of such a river and watched a procession of fishermen heading from one fast-flowing pool to the next. This makes sense, of course, for given the alternatives of sluggish-to-medium or medium-to-fast water, most salmon will settle on the latter. And these salmon do keep jumping and showing themselves.

A number of factors may cause salmon to jump. In this instance, it may be disturbance. A pool may hold a few more salmon than it has room for, which means that at least some of them are jostling to gain or hold a position. On hard-fished association water, fish may well be disturbed by a seemingly endless procession of floating lines and size 8 Munro Killers or Stoat's Tails passing over their heads. Whatever the cause, and with few exceptions, fish disturbed in either manner are not normally ready takers.

Then down comes a youngster or elderly angler who is dismissed as foolish to be fishing that slow stretch of water under the trees. But at the end of the day, when that unlikely stretch has produced the one and only fish, who is to say then that they were foolish. That particular salmon had set itself apart from the free-for-all of the open pools, gently holding station with its belly resting on a rock in slow-moving water close to a steep river bank beneath overhanging trees. It had not seen an artificial fly for some days. Then, suddenly, a tiny sparkling concoction of feather, floss and tinsel shimmered provocatively into view . . . "Would you believe it? He got it on a size 12 trout fly . . .".

Many fishermen seem to regard slow-flowing areas as worth fishing only when a river is high. Then the normally merry streams are transformed into raging torrents, and where the water normally appears almost dead, you have only to see a branch trailing in the water or a sheep's carcase floating past, or to set a foot in the current, to realise the speed at which it is moving. Not that you will need to set a foot in it – indeed, to do so would be dangerous – for the salmon will be lying fairly close to the bank, out of the full push of the current. That is why these normally slow-flowing stretches do give sport in times of spate; simply because they are the slowest-flowing and most sheltered parts of the river.

So long as the river remains high, and if you decide to keep to the fly, forget about floating lines and small flies. This is the time to reach for a long, double handed rod and fast-sinking line, with perhaps a 2-inch tube-fly. With plenty of colour still in the water, make a start with a fairly garish fly – perhaps a gold Mylar body with an orange wing including a few strands of red and yellow. As the water falls, you might do worse than try a Willie Gunn. And I might try my own Little's Secret Weapon – it would no longer be a secret if I said too much about it, other than that it is an indirect descendant of the Thunder and Lightning.

As the water falls and clears further, it reaches a transitional stage in which fairly standard, floating-line tactics may be used while the current has pace to swim the fly – perhaps a size 6 Shrimp Fly on the dropper and an 8 Garry Dog on the point. But soon the current is dying away, and these days it may be a matter of hours rather than days. I have fished on Hebridean waters where rain while I ate dinner brought a spate while I slept, a falling water before breakfast, and summer levels in the afternoon, and without sufficient current to swim the fly. So what now?

The answer, some of the time, is to strip-in line by hand, which immediately raises questions about tackle. Some anglers think only in terms of a sigle-handed rod when handlining is mentioned. Such a rod, of 10-11 ft, is certainly the most convenient and pleasant for the task in hand, and at the other end of the scale, a 15-footer is cumbersome. But what about the middle course?

Nowadays, I use my light, double-handed rod a lot in summer. It is 13 ft and handles 8 and 9 lines superbly, although when going for distance, and not casting in too contrary a wind, I do rig it with a 7 line. It gives me just that little bit extra in terms of water command; it Spey-casts efficiently with an 8 or 9 line when needed; and it is light enough to be used (if not necessarily cast) one-handed throughout the longest fishing day while the other hand concentrates on stripping line. It deals superbly with any three-winter salmon that might have sneaked upriver with the smaller summer fish and grilse, and for me is an extremely useful summer rod. But if you do prefer a single-handed rod, and derive most pleasure from its use, then, for goodness sake, don't let me sway you.

If an AFTM 8 rod is chosen, then 7 lb nylon will be safe. The difference between a 7 lb leader and one of 10 lb is often literally the difference between tempting a fish to take or causing it to shy away from the fly. Some folk regard salmon-fishing with leaders as light as 6 lb or 7 lb to be unjustified. It certainly is on a powerful 15 ft rod, but on a more sensitive wand, with a lightly set drag, it lets the angler give salmon the benefit of the doubt.

Many fishermen can recall times when a salmon took a fly on 6 lb nylon after showing no interest in the same tiny fly presented on stronger stuff. And off lines two fishermen of equal ability have fished together and one has caught more than the other, and the only apparent difference in tackle has been that one man was fishing 8 lb and his companion 12 lb. Similarly, and outwith summer fishing, I have known occasions when 12 lb or 14 lb nylon fished off the sunk line in clear water has scored, while 20 lb or heavier has failed. Anyone who is still

ROLLING OUT A DOUBLE-SPEY CAST OVER STEADY WATER. THE RIVER HAS CUT A DEEP CHANNEL ALONG THE SIDE OF THE RIVER BANK, AND THIS IS WHERE THE FISHER IS HOPING THAT A SALMON MAY LIE.

worried on this point should carry out the test which I described earlier of rigging up rod, reel, line and the desired breaking strain of leader, hooking the fly on to a strand of fence wire and trying to break the leader.

Slow, clear water in not normally the medium in which large flies are fished, especially when it is also warm. I would question the need for anything larger than a 10 on the point at such times, and I might choose even a 12. A tiny whisp of a tube-fly is a good alternative. The body, which may be electrical flex with the copper-wire core removed, need be only a quarter-of-an-inch long - giving barely enough room for a head when a sparse hairwing is tied on. Armed with a size 14, or even a 16, outpoint treble, this style of tube-fly really is deadly for fishing in slow-moving summer water, just as it is on a loch.

I sometimes wonder whether I shall ever find a fly that works quite as well as a Shrimp Fly for the dropper in this type of fishing, probably a size 10. Because of the Shrimp's long 'feelers', this fly, in terms of length, could be safely regarded as equivalent to an 8.

Sizes may be varied slightly according to water clarity and wind and wave. A breeze is a most valuable ally in fishing slow water. A good blow puts a ripple, even a wave, on the water, which serves to hide the fisherman and his rod and line. Here, if anywhere, and particularly on smaller flows, a strong case can be made for matt varnish on the rod, no flash about the reel, and a sober colour to the fly-line. (Use a white fly line if you must; it is up to you how many fish you catch!) An intermediate line, which avoids line wake, has great advantages over a floater. Do I seem, in this instance, to be against the use of white, floating lines?

Wind and wave offer another advantage in that I am convinced that they effectively stir up the fish and put them on the alert, making them far more likely to respond to a well-presented fly. Some fishermen prefer a downstream blow – it certainly helps in casting and presentation. Others, myself included, find that fish respond better in an upstream breeze – wind against flow.

How does one fish slow water? Let's consider what might be seen as a fairly typical salmon lie in these conditions. Many stretches of river have one bank that is steep and stable while the other shelves gently into the water. While wading would be possible for a good distance from the shelving bank, anyone who tried to wade off the steep bank would go straight over the top of his waders. In such places it is often the case that one bank has been reinforced, by tree roots or natural boulders, or by gabions, palings, wire mesh or ever-useful concrete, with the result that spate water has scoured out a channel hard against the steep bank while dropping gravel and sediment on the opposite shelving bank. Over the years, the channel becomes ever-deeper, until it is down to bed-rock, while the shelving side becomes ever-shallower. As a result, we quite properly wade off the shelving shore to present a fly to salmon seen in, or expected to be in, the deep channel.

Given insufficient current to swim the fly and give it life, it pays to strip-in line quite quickly following a squarish cast. A long, smooth draw on the line sometimes proves productive.

This method of fishing compares with fishing the lee-shore of a salmon loch. With one rod fishing, the gillie holds the boat so that the fisherman's cast lands hard in against the wave-washed boulders of the shoreline. Then the boat is pulled away with a clever stroke on the oars, and the fisherman keeps the retrieve going as the boat loses way by raising the tip of his rod and hand-lining. He speeds up the rate of his retrieve as the boat starts to drift back toward the shore, then makes another cast, and the process is repeated.

At other times, but less often, it seems that a jerky, almost sink-and-draw retrieve works

RUNNING LIES

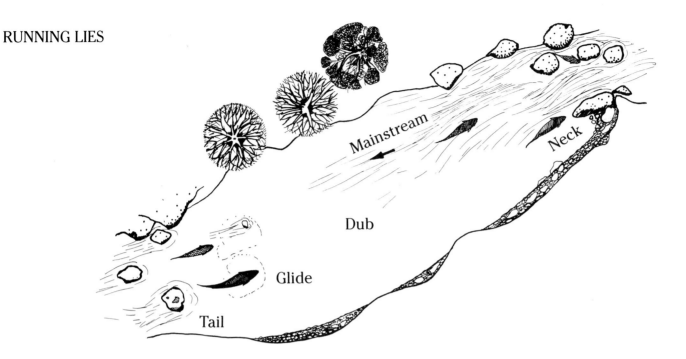

Running salmon will pause in the tails and glides of pools before moving up into the cheek of the mainstreams and on into the neck. These are the spots where the fisherman should concentrate his efforts.

best, particularly with the Shrimp Fly. The draws should be slow and about a foot at a time, with a distinct pause between each one.

It pays, as always, to vary tactics.

Once a slow stretch has been fished down in this way, it is as well to back up to the head of the pool which works just as well with the small flies of summer as it does with the larger flies associated with cold-water fishing. But it has to be said, that for some inexplicable reason, backing-up does better on some rivers than others.

The technique involves making a square cast, giving the flies and line a second or two to settle in the water, and then taking a few paces upstream, following this with some long draws on the line before repeating the process. Thus, fishing is upstream rather than down in terms of the direction in which the angler is moving.

Another technique of backing-up involves fishing in the conventional direction – downstream. The angler again makes a square cast, takes two upstream steps, drawing in line, and then takes four downstream steps, recovering line as he goes before making the next cast. Each technique is useful, but I prefer to move as little as possible and in just one direction, rather than indulging in a lot of to-ing and fro-ing which might disturb the fish.

It always pays to be discreet in moving about the banks, staying off the skyline and wading quietly rather than like a water buffalo. I remember fishing in the Hebrides with my father and watching him slither and slide his way down a high bank, slip into the water like an otter, and creep along like a stalking heron, dressed from head to toe in drab greens and browns and shod in felt-soled waders. It was an absolute treat to watch the way he delicately flicked out his fly on a light trout rod. A small salmon rolled lazily on the surface, just where the next cast was likely to land . . ..

And then our host, clad in a bright shirt, came stomping up, stood on the skyline, shouted down that father would disturb the fish by wading down there, and stomped off again.

I looked at my father's face. Dismissing the passing worry that it might be difficult to find a coronary-care unit in such a remote spot, I had almost to stuff my mouth with heather to stop myself laughing out loud and just rolled about in silent mirth. Father, to this day has never seen the funny side of it. To be honest, I don't think that I would if it happened to me.

THE APPROACH TO SLOW FLOWS

High Water: Normally slow-flowing stretches offer shelter to salmon during times of high water. Salmon will lie fairly close to the bank, as a general rule. Use a long, double-handed rod and a sinking line to 'hover' a big, bright fly – perhaps an Orange-and-yellow on a 2-inch tube – right in to the bank.

Falling water: Salmon may move to flies fished off a floating line as the water falls and clears, but maintains an adequate flow to fish flies in conventional manner. A size 6 or 8 Shrimp Fly is worth a try on the dropper, with an 8 or 10 Garry, Munro Killer or Silver Stoat on the point.

Low water: The outstanding feature of slow-water stretches in times of low water is that the current is insufficient to fish a fly effectively if it is left to its own devices. Choose a single-handed rod of about 10 ft, or a light double-hander of about 13 ft, partnered with an intermediate line to avoid line-wake, and fish tiny flies on light leaders. Cast squarely and draw line and fly back, either by stripping-in or backing-up.

Wind: A breeze to ruffle the surface also conceals anglers' antics and is a great advantage on slow-flowing water. A downstream breeze is most comfortable for casting, but an upstream blow may produce more fish.

BRIGHT FLIES ARE OFTEN FAVOURED IN SPATE WATER – HERE IS THE AUTHOR'S OWN 'JUNGLE BUCK' IN STANDARD AND LONG-WING ALTERNATIVES. THE DRESSING IS AS FOLLOWS: TAG – OVAL GOLD, TAIL – YELLOW BUCKTAIL, BODY – BLACK FLOSS, RIB – GOLD, WING – ORANGE, CHEEKS – JUNGLE-COCK, HEAD – BLACK.

CHAPTER EIGHT

August

SALMON IN A SPATE

A lure, fly or spinner, seems to swim more attractively on a medium-to-long line. It certainly fishes more slowly. A long line should be laid downstream at an angle of less than 45 degrees . . . with fly a big mend should be made the moment the sinking line alights on the water. With the rod pointed at the opposite bank, the fly will eventually hang straight downstream . . . hanging for a few seconds . . . Then a salmon hammers in . . ..

With the river running high and clear, I reached for my 16 ft rod and rigged it with a fast-sinking line and big fly. Tail-end of summer or not, this was neither the time nor the place for a sensitive, small-fly-and-floating-line approach. The tube that formed the base of the fly was copper. It was dressed with a black floss body ribbed with broad flat and oval gold tinsels, laid in parallel. The wing was principally orange, broken by strands of yellow and red. With jungle-cock cheeks and a red tulip bead to take the eye of the size 4 treble, it was an eye-catching pattern.

A leader of only 6 ft of 15 lb nylon kept the fly short-tethered to the fast-sinking line, but gave it enough play to fish with a lively action in the strong stream. In slacker water, I might have chosen an aluminium tube. Either way, in this particular instance I knew that I had made the right choice, because it allowed me to fish the fly right round into the bank without it snagging on the bottom.

A good, long rod such as my 16-footer can pay handsome dividends when a river comes down in spate. The angler can stay dry and safe on the bank, but still be able to hang and hover the fly over the noses of any salmon that have moved right into the bank in search of shelter. I sometimes choose my 17-footer, which allows me to mend line in enormous upstream loops. Then I simply point it at the opposite shore and let the fly dangle.

This static fly-fishing can almost be compared to harling. Harling, in which a boat is moved slowly back and forth across the river, dropping slowly downstream while trailing a selection of flies and spinners in the current, can be mind-numbingly boring, but it kills great numbers of salmon. A really light tube fished on a fast-sinking line can be made to copy the erratic and fish-attractive movements of lures such as the Toby and Kynoch Killer. Whatever and whichever, a long fly-rod enabled a fly to be hovered in to the bank on which the angler is standing. And it keeps him safe. Being tempted to step on an undercut bank when the river is in high spate can be, at worst, a deadly experience.

The hanging, hovering fly works well with running fish when a spate starts to fall away. A salmon may be edging its way upstream and pause in a slight eddy for a breather, only to discover it is sharing it with a bright but demented object that buzzes about its heads – at least, that is what I imagine to happen in the moments before the rod bows and the reel speaks.

A long, fairly supple rod acts as a cushion to fish taking in this position, and I strive to maintain as great an angle as possible between rod and line, and perhaps create extra 'droop' in the line by holding the rod-tip up at a slight angle to act as a buffer to a taking salmon. Even the best of trebles can fail to find a secure hold, and if a salmon comes screaming up to the surface, it has probably been tipped on its nose, and the chances are the fish will be lost. In such an event, I pile on the pressure anyway. It is better to lose a fish at the start of the fight than to exhaust him so that he no longer has the strength to hold his own in heavy, rolling spate water.

If this approach to catching salmon is thought 'rough and ready', I can only say that I learned it from a master of the old school. He was a gillie, and something of a hero to me in my younger years. At times I must have worn his patience to a sharp point.

He gillied the beat that had been his father's, and his father's father before him. He was not a particularly big man, but he had great strength and stamina. If he had a fault, it was one which I recognised only with hindsight: he expected all his guests to show comparable reserves of energy. The thought never crossed my mind at the time, but it must have been irksome for some of the middle-aged and elderly fishers to find themselves the object of his unspoken wrath should they be caught resting when fish were there to be caught. He was not slow to signal his disapproval of the spinning rod, nor of the man who used one. Ladies and children were excused on this point; but only them.

His clear but unspoken prejudice possibly carried a degree of method. Males who had passed beyond their mid-teens had two basic options when they tired of handling the long rod and heavy tackle: they could either spend time with the spinning rod (in which case they were certain to incur the gillie's wrath), or they could suggest that he should fish their rod for a while (which would bring a smile of delight to his face and ensure, when they resumed fishing, that he would be at their elbow with a wealth of invaluable advice). In such circumstances, men catch on remarkably quickly as to what is expected of them!

If we were some distance from the fishing hut, he would accept the cane or fibre-glass rod he was offered. (Remember, this was back in the days before carbon had come on the scene.) But if we were close to the hut, with its rod box, he would stroll back to fetch his own tackle. If he was sure fish were there to be caught, he might actually scamper there and back. He would return and go in at the head of the stretch without a word. His thoughts were only for the fishing.

His rod was a treat to behold. It was a 17 or 18 ft Grant Vibration green–heart, and it had been his grandfather's. The reel, presented to his father by a grateful guest at the end of a fantastic week of spring fishing, was a $4\frac{1}{2}$-inch Hardy Perfect. My hero's only contribution, beside the leader and fly, was one of the then new plastic sinking lines, which caused him to swear a lot.

His casting style was hardly artistic, but it was certainly effective – and awe-inspiring. Indeed, one of his gripes about modern lines was that, at 30 yards, they were too short. His attitude to having to strip-in and subsequently shoot a lot of line was akin to his notions on spinning. He was one of the first exponents of the Spey cast I ever saw. That was something else he had learned from his father, and his grandfather, and I can still picture the long line shooting far out across the river. It went out dead-straight, regardless of the wind, in a way that I could never hope to match with my 14 ft glass rod.

I never heard him say anything against the tube-fly, but he relied on the traditionally huge and heavy single salmon iron, or 'meat hook' which I referred to them as when I thought he was out of earshot.

It was he who taught me to fish the big fly slow and deep. He saw fishing as fishing, rather than a punctuation mark between casts, and he took just as long as he wanted over fishing out each and every cast. His face would be rapt with concentration when fishing a high water and the fly came edging its way toward salmon's resting places, and he never failed to hang his fly for a few long moments, then give three – and always three – long, slow draws on the line before quickly stepping downstream and making his next cast.

One funny habit he developed for a time was to quickly mutter, "Na", at the end of each swim of the fly, if it had failed to move a fish. I never said anything about it, but perhaps somebody embarrassed him with a thoughtless remark, for he had dropped the habit when next I saw him. However, he was never inhibited from giving a running commentary on the parentage and habits of a fish throughout the fairly short time it took him to bring one to a standstill on that old but still powerful rod. But back to salmon in spate. . . .

Why have I chosen August as the month in which to discuss spates? The fact is that I caught my first salmon on the heels of an August spate! And even in the driest of summer, we can usually expect rain and spates at some time during the month. On some Highland waters, they may provide the last real sport before the season's close. In the border country, from Solway Firth to Tweedside, they are seen as harbingers of the great autumn runs that take sport through to the end of November on Nith and Tweed.

But rivers are in spate at virtually any time of the season, and you perhaps know the old rhyme:

> *Sometimes ower early, sometimes ower late.*
> *Sometimes nae watter, sometimes a spate.*
> *There's aye something wrang when I am fishing here.*

Heaven knows, there are plenty of times in a season when we find ourselves thinking that!

Spates affect different rivers in different ways. Think of the Spey in, say, late April. The water is holding at a steady fishing height under the influence of snow melting on the mountains. Then come a few days of rain, adding accelerated snowmelt to their own rise in water. It virtually puts an end to thoughts of productive fishing. High spates on the Tweed can find anglers praying for an overnight frost to 'close the tap' on the run-off. Closest to my own home, the Nith is severely affected by spates that run the colour of clay for days. Then the water starts to fall, and out come the worming rods. Then it falls a little further, and the wormers are joined by spinners. Finally, with the water about an inch above low summer level, the fly-only rule is enforced. (Perhaps I exaggerate. It could be two inches above low-water mark.) Then within a day or two, catches have faded away.

Compare the heights of these spates (their peaks associated with a definite scarcity of fish)

NOW THAT THE RIVER IS FALLING AND CLEARING, SALMON WILL BE MOVING UPSTREAM. AS THE SPATE FALLS AWAY, AND SALMON ARE RUNNING AND PAUSING ON THEIR UPSTREAM JOURNEY, FISHING CHANCES ARE AT THEIR BEST.

PLAYING A SALMON IN A SPATE-COLOURED RIVER. KEEPING THE ROD POINT RAISED ALLOWS THE FISH TO RUN AND PUTS MINIMUM STRAIN ON THE HOOK-HOLD.

with what can happen on a river such as the Aberdeenshire Dee. The start of a rise follows the general pattern of a brief flurry of activity, followed by a lull in sport. But the Dee seldom remains hopeless for more than a relatively short time, when the rise in level is well underway. Where the Dee does differ is that, after the initial rise, it can start, and continue, to fish well on a really high water. This was proved back in 1983, which saw the wettest spring in more than 40 years. Anglers found the river exceptionally high, but clear. Why should this be so? Is it down simply to the renowned clarity of the Dee?

It was Richard Waddington who suggested that the reason for sport coming to a standstill in some rivers at times of spate, while it continued on others, depended upon a chemical factor in the water. He felt that water in those rivers where spates had devastating long-term effects upon the fishing was strongly acidic.

Whether this theory has ever been proved, I don't know, but now that we are all aware of the effects of acid rain, it certainly gives food for thought. Instances are known of fish-stocks of a river being exterminated by high acidity. This occurred on the Cumbrian Esk, although it is said now to be slowly recovering. Whatever the arguments, one fact is that certain rivers do not show sport at the *peak* of a spate, while others do. This prospect should at least receive the benefit of the doubt before fishermen head for home or retire to the hotel bar.

Having decided not to throw in the towel just yet, the first thing to be considered is where salmon are likely to be encountered. We know they will seek shelter out of the main force of the current, but it is possible to be more exact.

The first place that I would turn to when seeking salmon in a spate would be on an inside curve of the river where a jumble of rocks and boulders is strewn in fairly deep water close to the bank. It obviously helps if the river has been reconnoitred in low water. The surface in spate may well be turbulent and seem not to offer much shelter, but I picture salmon lying in one of the small pockets of shelter right down among the boulders. Salmon seem to like nothing more than to fin gently in a pocket of quiet water with fast water all around, preferably with their bellies pressed flat on to a slab of rock by just the right ease in the current. Experienced fishermen are familiar with the abrasions on a salmon's belly and chin associated with the aftermath of high water.

The bank on the other side of the river is exposed to the full force of the current pushing into the outside curve, so it is on the sheltered, inside curve that fish may be found. The aim must be to fish the lure, be it tube-fly or spinner, slowly and tantalisingly, and right into the bank. Fishing up to the bank on a spate water is crucial in deciding the depth at which to fish, and thus the tackle chosen. Handling the fly, or cranking the spinning reel, to avoid catching the bottom shouldn't be necessary.

Anyone who chooses to mix fly-fishing with spinning should find that a buoyant wooden Devon minnow, with a small weight above the swivel, some 2 ft up the trace, serves well. A light fly, fished off a fast-sinking line, gives a similar effect. The lead may bump the bottom, but the buoyant minnow will swim above it, and may be very productive.

My choice would be to start with a fly-rod. Only if this failed, would I try the spinner. Incidentally, spinning rods of 8–9 ft are not ideal for this type of work. They don't have the length needed to hang and hover a lure over the salmon's resting places. I would use a 12-footer. This seems a bit of a beast, but, in carbon, it is certainly not too heavy to handle.

It's as well to stand well upstream of the spot to be covered. A lure, fly or spinner, seems to swim more attractively on a medium-to-long line. It certainly fishes more slowly. A long line should be laid downstream at an angle of less than 45 degrees. Remember, the salmon are close to the bank, so what is the point of wasting time in fishing the central rush? With fly, a big mend should be used the moment the line alights on the water, and not a second later with a sinking line. This again helps the fly to fish as slowly as possible.

With the rod pointed at the opposite bank, the lure will eventually hang straight downstream from the rod-tip. It can be left hanging for a few seconds, and then, with a spinner, retrieved slowly with four or five turns of the reel handle. With fly, the hand should reach right up to the butt-ring of the rod, grasp the line, and sweep back in one long, straight pull. "Na!". If the piscatorial version of the auctioneer's "going, going, gone" hasn't tempted a fish this time, then it's time for a pace downstream and the next cast.

But the time comes when a salmon hammers in with a last-second snatch. And 'snatch' is often the operative word. A fish taking straight downstream on the dangle is reported to be the hardest of all to hook. The rod should never be pointed straight down the line. If the fly or spinner has to be led across to bring it close into the bank, as may be necessary on the inside curve, the rod-tip should be kept well up to create some droop in the line and to allow the action of the rod to act as a cushion to the snatchy pull. That is another argument against the use of short, stiff rods.

It has been said that salmon will lie in backwaters at times of spate. This is a half-truth. I have never caught a salmon from an area of contra-flow, but salmon will certainly rest just downstream of such an area, where the water gathers into a strong gliding run back into the mainstream – and they can be caught. However, such a position is not easily fished. From the near bank, it is necessary to cast over the area of contra-flow, and then the line comes snaking back toward the angler, who probably gives up in disgust. Another option is to cross to the other side of the river, if possible and if the new position is still within casting range.

I came upon just such a backwater and glide one August morning on a West Highland river. A salmon was moving at the head of the glide, but, despite my best efforts, I couldn't cover him, at least not effectively. Ten minutes later, with my rod clamped on the roof, I was driving up the glen to cross the nearest bridge – five miles up and five miles back down on the opposite bank of the high, unfordable river.

My longest cast and a fairly enormous upstream mend to counteract the strong central current tearing at the belly of the line was needed before I was satisfied that the fly was fishing attractively. Third cast down and a *click, click, click* came from the reel. Was it a sunken twig, cartwheeling down the spate? The reel began to accelerate. It could be a fertiliser bag. Then came a fine old scream from the reel and a whirring reel handle. I clamped the line and raised the rod into a hard tussle with what eventually proved to be a beautifully fresh fish. Shortly afterwards, I had its twin. Both had sucked the big orange-and-yellow tube-fly back to a secure hold, deep in their throats. The total drive of 20 miles, 10 there and 10 back for lunch, seemed more than worthwhile.

To fish a big fly during a spate in exciting work. True, the fish caught are no more than a prelude to what can be expected when the water has fallen and cleared. But salmon *can* be caught, and on the fly, and this is particularly important to the angler on holiday who may have to return home before the river really comes into its own. It is certainly better to give a fly a swim, rather than sit on a rock or bar-stool reciting, "Sometimes ower early, sometimes ower late".

This description of sport in a spate shouldn't be taken to imply that high, coloured water is

A SPATE WATER SALMON COMES TO THE AUTHOR'S NET. A NET SHOULD ALWAYS BE CARRIED AT SUCH TIMES, BECAUSE IT CAN BE DANGEROUS TO GET INTO THE WATER TO HAND-TAIL THE FISH.

conducive to good fishing. It isn't. But a fish or two may be caught by anyone prepared to persevere.

Richard Waddington's suggestion that it is the acidity of spate water, varying from river to river, as well as from time to time, which affects the fishing may well be correct, but few of us carry a *p*H kit. It might not be a bad idea if we did, but meantime, a lot may be deduced by inspecting a river.

A number of Highland rivers give the appearance of being fishable immediately after the height of a spate. They do not colour up in the same way as lowland rivers running through arable land, but they do suffer from 'black' spates. These are reminiscent of a glass of Irish stout – black with a creamy foam on top. The foam tells us a lot, and fishing is unlikely to be at all good until it has cleared. Then we look for the flotsam and jetsam of twigs and branches to disappear.

Spates on lowland rivers really do test an angler's patience. I live on the Solway, where salmon rivers flow off high hills covered by forestry plantations and their associated drainage schemes. Lord Home compared the effect of these with rain falling on roofs of slate or thatch. In the old days, the open hills were the equivalent of the thatched roof, and the rivers rose and fell in a sedate manner, maintaining a good fishing height over an extended period. But when the hillsides were striped with open drains as a prelude to forestry planting they became the equivalent of a slate roof, with the water running off quickly to cause flash floods with rapid rise and fall. The fishing has suffered severely as a result.

And what will happen when the forests are more mature? The drains will block, and with ranks upon ranks of thirsty trees, the headwater streams, the nursery areas for salmon and sea-trout, will dry out completely in dry summers and the big spates that serve to cleanse the river will become less and less frequent . . . no, from the fishing point of view, there is little if any good to be said for modern, commercial forestry.

This is not the place to enter into a discussion on the future of the Scottish uplands, but when one looks at the grants and subsidies enjoyed by hill-farmers over the years, and the unprecedented financial incentives for forestry which have attracted so many unlikely investors to add a slice of wild places to their portfolios, is it not odd that the only financial aspect of sport is that it contributes through the payment of rates? It is past time that the decision-makers were made to sit up, take notice and realise that the income and employment created by sport with rod, rifle and gun is so vital to many rural economies that they should be thinking about giving back just some of what they take. . . .

What else of lowland spates? They see traffic slowed to a crawl over Tweed bridges thronged with frustrated fishermen and boatmen, peering over the parapets, searching for the merest hint that the river is falling and clearing. Prayers are offered for an overnight frost to shut down the run-off from forestry schemes, bankside fields and road washings, that the river may drop a few feet and, above all, clear, so that we can all get back to fishing with confidence.

Salmon need spates to run the rivers just as we need them to bring fresh fish into the beat we are fishing. We may be "ower early" or "ower late" to benefit as individuals. But, while "nae watter" is a near-perfect excuse, "sometimes a spate" is something for which we should be truly grateful.

FLY DRESSING STYLE AND PROPORTIONS

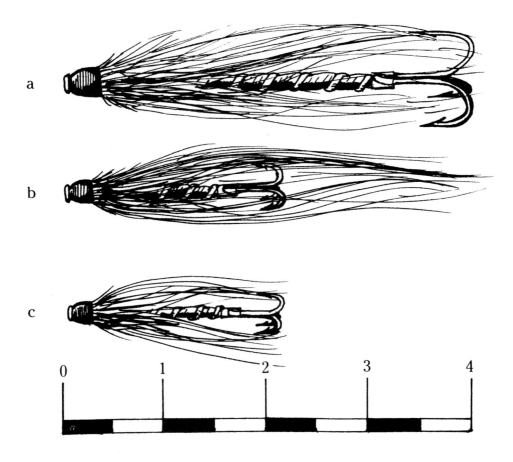

a) The standard dressing – a 4 inch tube fly dressed on a 3 inch tube

b) The author's preference – a 4 inch tube fly dressed on a 1½ or 2 inch tube – puts the weight where it should be, and creates very attractive stimulus

c) A standard dressing on a short tube for comparison

CHAPTER NINE

September

A Funny Sort of a Time

The tempo increases with each passing week. These late-running fish do not hang about. They stem spates and take obstructions in conditions that would hold back springers . . . We do well to regard late-summer and autumn salmon as sleek, active torpedo-like fish, and autumn salmon fishing as being concerned with intercepting hard-running fish. The end-result can be some of the most exciting fishing experiences imaginable.

September can be an odd time on the salmon river, particularly when the equinoctial rains and gales cause the river to rise and the water temperature to fall. We can all become just a little bit confused. So much of our present-day salmon thinking is still based on what worked best back in the days when the springer was king. Look at the history of beats such a Delfur on the Spey. In the 1950s and 1960s the five rods could expect to average about 20 springers day after day. Fishing such as this obviously moulded the thinking of the now older generation of salmon fishermen, and because it is from them that the younger generation has learned, the rules set in the past have continued into the present, and no doubt will continue into the future.

It is tempting to regard autumn salmon fishing as nothing more than a mirror image of the sport we once enjoyed in the spring, before the pattern of runs moved so dramatically from spring to late summer and autumn. This may be a mistake, as I will explain later. For now, let me just say that early-season and late-season sport show as many subtle differences as they do similarities.

If we do seek to impose spring rules on autumn fishing, we find ourselves keeping with the floating line and small fly until the water temperature has dropped below 50 degrees Fahrenheit. Then we will change to a fast-sinking line and a 2-inch tube-fly. Both methods will catch fish, and plenty of them. But neither of them will meet all needs at all places and all times. But major changes and some fairly minor changes will reap handsome rewards.

Why should differences exist between the behaviour of spring and autumn salmon? To answer that, we need to take a closer look at the fish.

Salmon that return in the winter and spring of the year tend to be lethargic. January and February are usually the coldest months of the year, and salmon entering the rivers at this

WHEN THE LEAVES START TO FALL, MANY FISHERMEN GET OUT THEIR SPINNING RODS. EARLY AUTUMN ON THE RIVER NITH, BELOW THE TOWN OF SANQUHAR, DUMFRIESSHIRE.

time often do no more than creep into the lowermost pools, showing great reluctance to go further while the river water remains so much colder than the sea. Because of its comparative lack of volume and depth, river water cools more quickly than does the sea in winter; equally, it warms up faster in summer. Salmon will not attempt to surmount any obstacles until the water temperature has reached the lower 40s, which is why, for example, the fishing on the Helmsdale is confined to beats below Kildonan Falls during the opening months of the season. Winter and spring salmon are in no rush; why should they be?

Many long months have to pass before they have an appointment to keep on the spawning redds. In fact, their behaviour *must* be centred on the need to conserve energy. They are not feeding, so they must avoid unnecessary activity and so conserve the energy contained in their flesh to see them through the long months of summer. That is why, with notable exceptions, such as a shallow-swimming Collie fly, we concentrate our fishing effort on presenting early-season fish with a large fly, fished deep and slow and virtually hovering in front of the fish so that they can, if so moved, suck it in with minimum effort. The life of winter- and spring-running fish must be that of the tortoise, rather than the hare.

Contrast this with salmon returning in late summer and autumn, from September, say, through to the end of the autumn runs. The tempo increases with each passing week. These late running fish do not hang about. They stem spates and take obstructions at temperatures that would hold back springers. With spawning so close, nothing is going to get in their way. And, of course, they may not run as high upstream as springers do. Early fish tend to make a sedate passage to the headwaters and tributaries. Autumn fish are just as likely to choose the middle and lower river. On a clear day, and with polarising glasses, spawning salmon can be seen beneath the bridge at Kelso.

We do well to regard late-summer and autumn salmon as sleek, active, torpedo-like fish, and autumn salmon fishing as being concerned with intercepting hard-running fish as they pause to rest. Our aim should be to present a pattern or design of lure which will stimulate an aggressive or predatory response. The end-result can be some of the most exciting fishing experiences imaginable.

To write about the interception of running fish seems at odds with long-established lore of salmon-fishing. Tradition is that running fish will not take. I believe this to be just another of those half-truths. I will go further and say that most of the salmon we catch in a season are in fact runners – or, to be a little more accurate, in the *process* of running. Salmon simply do not make a headlong dash up through the pools of a river. Far from it. Even autumn fish, which tend to be the fastest runners of all, pause in the tails of certain pools before moving up and on to the dub, where they may linger in the cheeks of the main stream before cruising up to the neck of the pool, again pausing before scurrying up the rough water into the tail of the next pool.

The time fish actually spend in a pool depends on a host of factors, not least water height. It may be days, hours or weeks. And the times at which we are most likely catch them is just as they are settling into a lie, and again as they are about to move on to the next temporary lodging. In a run or stream, they may pause for moments, minutes or hours in an area of shelter which may be little larger than a table-top.

Salmon tend to keep running upstream just as long as the water height remains suitable, or until they reach a spawning redd. But how do we set about catching them? The answer, related to a number of rivers fished throughout the back-end months, encompasses virtually all known salmon-catching techniques, and a few more besides.

In September, everything is rather less predictable because it is often toward the end of this month, with its associated equinoctial rain and gales, that the thermometer drops below 50 degrees. We can become thoroughly confused in trying to decide when to set aside the floating line and take up the sinker. It is easy to write that we should make the change at 50 degrees. But fishermen with more precise intellects will recall the advice of Arthur Wood's disciples and make the change when the water temperature reaches 48 degrees, on the dot. This, however, shows nothing more than that we seek to impose a mirror-image of spring experiences on what we find in autumn; what goes up must come down.

Equally, the water temperature may hover at about 50 degrees for some time. It may have dropped to the mid-40s when we set out in the morning, only to rise into the 50s at midday and fall back in the evening.

My own practice is that while I will keep with the sinking line in spring until the water temperature is fairly steady above 50 degrees Fahrenheit, I will not return to the sinker in autumn until the temperature has fallen and steadied below 45 degrees. High water might have me changing that little bit later or sooner, in spring or autumn respectively. And on a day of wildly fluctuating temperatures, nothing would stop me starting with a sunk line and big fly early in the day, swopping to a floater and smaller fly while the sun warms the river, and then swopping back to a sinker in the cool of the evening.

When the Nith had its record season, in 1988, it was September that produced most fish. October is normally the best month, but water levels favoured an early start to autumn sport. Temperature also played its part, for I had most of my salmon by what might be regarded almost as classic floating-line methods. I remember lightly-clouded skies and high midday temperatures. Never be too quick to presume, on a falling temperature but with clear water, that the floating line has lost its appeal. Remember the active nature of autumn fish.

I remember coming home a few years ago at the start of October to find the Solway rivers running high but surprisingly clear. The water temperature was in the lower 40s. I started fishing with a fast-sinking line and big tube-fly and caught a fish on the Tuesday morning. That evening, however, a man who practically lives on the river told me of the sport he was still enjoying on the floating line, insisting that I should give it a try. Next morning found me fishing a 1-inch tube, similar to a Willie Gunn, and using the floater. Success was immediate and sustained.

I do not normally fish a heavy fly off a high line, but choose instead a lighter tube or a long-winged Esmond Drury-type pattern and hook fished above an intermediate to achieve the same depth. The differences might be thought academic, but I have already set out my own reasoning (Chapter 5) which gives some idea as to when I might set aside the floater and give the intermediate a swim. Fishing is surely, within reason, a personal affair, involving the tackle and techniques in which we have most faith, which we enjoy using, and which give us best results. I do not see the intermediate as an out-and-out alternative to the floater, far more as a partner to be fished as mood or conditions suggest. Let me relate another experience which will perhaps give a clearer picture.

I had been fishing a floating line and relatively small flies – size 8 Stinchar Stoat's and the like. Friday, however, had been a washout, with the river rising after rain. Saturday saw the river still high and dirty, so I gave it a rest.

I was down at the river quite early on Monday. A fair breeze was blowing and, while conditions did not look right for the floating line and small fly, the water temperature was back up in the mid-40s, so I was hesitant to use sunk-line technique. Some fishermen might have dug out their sink-tips lines, but as I don't like them, I decided to pin my faith on the intermediate.

Now the intermediate can be used in a number of ways. It can be used – wrongly in my opinion – to present a heavy fly in mid-water; or it can be used to present a fairly light fly within the top 6 inches or so of the river; or it can fish a medium-weight fly about 1ft below the surface. Do I seem to be splitting hairs again?

Anyone who has fished on salmon and sea-trout lochs will be aware that some winds produce good fishing, while others do not. Warm, soft, steady blows from the south and west should see both salmon and sea-trout coming to the surface to take a tripping, dibbling bob-fly. But let the wind come out of the north or east and you may soon be fastening another button on your jacket and realising that the fish are either no longer interested in the surface fly or are coming short. Much the same experience can be had on rivers. Doubtless there are

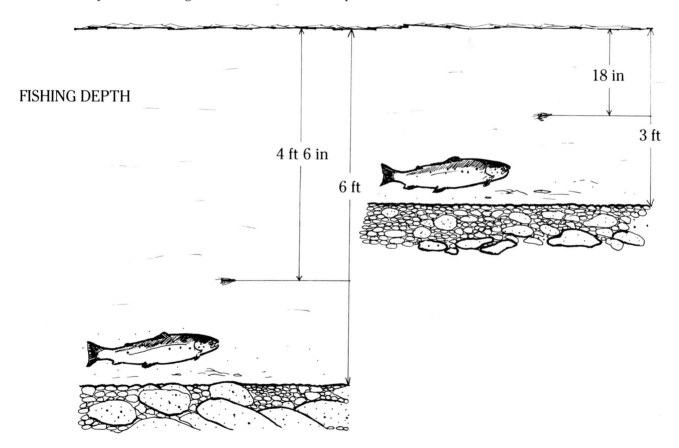

FISHING DEPTH

18 in

3 ft

4 ft 6 in

6 ft

Should be largely decided by considering the depth of the stream in which the salmon are lying

CHOOSING A FLY – SALMON FISHING IN SEPTEMBER CAN BE THOUGHT PROVOKING, PARTICULARLY WHEN THE WATER TEMPERATURE IS FLUCTUATING WILDLY. THE OPTIONS, POSSIBILITIES AND PERMUTATIONS OF LIGHT AND HEAVY FLIES, A FLOATING OR ONE OF A RANGE OF SINKING LINES, NEEDS CLOSE CONSIDERATION.

exceptions, but my thinking is that salmon do not respond nearly so well to a fly fished close to the surface when a cold, squally wind is blowing as they do when a warmer wind is blowing. Sometimes, it is necessary to fish right down to get a response. At other times, the fly need be only a touch deeper, but still *relatively* close to the surface.

I rummaged through my fly-boxes and found what I was looking for – a Black-and-orange with short, jungle-cock cheeks. I had tied it on one of my home-produced variants of the Waddington shank, using brass wire. The shank was barely 1 inch long, then came the size 8 treble, while the wing trailed back to a point some distance behind. I do like a longish wing, and tear-drop shape on this style of fly. Such a fly has weight, but is not heavy. And its weight is in the right place to cause it to swim on an even keel.

I was soon up to my thighs in water at the top of a grand, fly-fishing stream. A child could wade it in safety, so long as he was not tempted to go out too far on the shingle. Further out, the increasing depth and force of the current can take you by surprise, but there is no need to go so far as that to cover fish effectively, with the fly coming over them long before it hangs on the first dangle. A line of trees halfway down the pool might push an overhead caster toward midstream, but they can be ignored by a Spey-caster.

I fished the pool down without moving a fin, but that did nothing to remove the feeling that salmon were there to be caught. So I walked back up and started to fish down for a second time.

I wondered whether I had allowed the fly to fish just a little too quickly first time down, so I waded further out toward the 'danger' area and concentrated on throwing a longer line across the stream to allow it time and scope to reach the desired depth. I mended, hung, then led the fly across – and finished with two salmon before lunch and one after, all by the same techniques and on the same line-fly combination on that fine September day.

SUCCESS IN SEPTEMBER

Conditions: September, like May, is a month of change. Water temperatures may be rising and falling either side of 50 degrees Fahrenheit, often accepted as the changeover point between smaller, shallow-swimming flies, and the deep, slow presentation of larger flies.

Solutions: It can be hard, on a day-to-day basis, to be specific as to what technique to choose. So long as the water temperature is still above 45 degrees, and conditions seem appropriate for the floating line (see Chapter 5), make a start with this option, fishing perhaps a size 6 Munro Killer or Stinchar Stoat. If conditions are not so good, try the same flies off an intermediate line.

Once the water temperature is below 45 degrees, start to think about the larger flies fished off a sinking line. Keep your mind and options open. When fish are running, concentrate your efforts on the neck, cheeks of the mainstream, and the glide and tail of the pool; and remember that a large, 3-inch total-length Waddington can work well at intercepting runners that pause for a breather. It can be fished conventionally, or high and fast following a square cast.

FISHING THE SHOOTING HEAD

Wishing line and fly 'bon voyage'

Double taper

Shooting head with oval nylon shooting line

The shooting head goes down really deep

On the lower Tweed beats, with slow deep dubs, the fast sinking shooting head is a very effective method for achieving depth and distance.

CHAPTER TEN

October

HARVEST OF THE SCOTTISH BORDERS

You can spend thousands of pounds on renting a middle Tweed beat in October or November. Your tackle can see off another thousand, and you are likely to spend a large amount on travel, hotel and bar bills, boatmen's tips and the like. But all the salmon cares about is the concoction of floss, fur, tinsel and metal and plastic that you swim across its nose. The way that the fly is presented is important, but, surely, we cannot think that the size, pattern and design of the fly are irrelevant?

I live on the Solway Firth. The rivers of the area produce tremendous runs of autumn salmon. In fact, were it not for this autumn fishing, local rivers, such as the Border Esk, Annan, Nith and other less-spoken-about waters, would be known only for their summer sea-trout. But these rivers produce an annual autumn harvest running to many thousands of fish.

For most salmon-fishers, however, autumn fishing is more strongly associated with Tweed. There, as on Nith, the season goes through to the end of November. Salmon run fast, clean and in their tens of thousands up to and beyond this date. Make no mistake: salmon see no reason to be limited by any statutory restrictions as imposed on mere men. They keep pouring into the rivers right into winter. On late November days, too, we may find the earliest springers featuring in our bags. Yes, they are springers, because gutting them reveals that the spawn is barely formed.

I do not have to consult my fishing diary to know that October and November are the most hectic times of my fishing season. I have to plan ahead and travel for much of my spring and summer sport, in autumn it is right here on my doorstep; or, if I have an appointment on Tweed, a relatively short drive away. So do not be surprised to find me with a gleam in my eye at this time of the year.

It is easy to paint an overly rosy picture of back-end sport. Sure, we may enjoy a bonanza if conditions are right, but often enough they are not right. They may alternate between bitter gales and high, cold floods, or perhaps combine the two. But, as they say in the Borders, they sort out the men from the boys.

To increase the challenge for Tweedsiders, the rule there is that fishing is by fly only after

ROD, REELS, LINES AND A SELECTION OF FLIES FOR THE SCOTTISH BORDER HARVEST-TIME. LATE IN THE SEASON, SALMON IN THEIR THOUSANDS SWIM UP FROM THE SEA TO TWEED AND ITS TRIBUTARIES IN THE EAST, AND THE SOLWAY AND AYRSHIRE RIVERS IN THE WEST.

A BOX FULL OF AUTUMNAL PATTERNS TIED ON WADDINGTON AND BRORA SHANKS. POPULAR PATTERNS INCLUDE THE BLACK AND YELLOW,. BLACK AND ORANGE, WILLIE GUNN, COMET AND WHITEWING.

mid-September. That makes things particularly difficult when a contrary wind is blowing, but doesn't sport, by definition, include the meeting of challenges? It means, too, that we must pay utmost attention to our choice of tackle if we are to be able to face whatever comes along.

It is easy to write that on a calm, sunny summer evening, with the scent of fresh-cut grass on the air. Perhaps I should be more realistic, because autumn fishing can be damned hard work. Sometimes the challenge simply cannot be met with any real hope of success. After some days with the long rod, sinking line and heavy fly, I have found myself soaking in the bath and wondering whether I ached more or less when I toiled against Tweedside's rugby teams rather than its salmon.

But, it is not always so, and in the Indian summer of a warm October we may still be fishing with a floating or intermediate line and relatively small flies. More usually, however, it is the more powerful tackle to which we resort. It may be hard work at times, but it can be wildly productive and, infinitely more pleasureable than fishing spinner or worm, so often used on the Solway.

I have a theory about the question of fly *versus* other methods. It is based on my belief that, within a given number of salmon, a certain proportion will be almost definite takers, a rather large number probables, a still larger group possibles, and the largest group of all, those that never will take, whatever is offered. I suspect that what happens is that when a new batch of salmon comes in on the heels of a spate, with the wormers out in force, the 'definites' and some of the 'probables' are seen off pretty quickly. The water continues to fall and has almost cleared when the spinners take their toll, clearing up the remainder of the 'probables' and biting into the 'possibles'. The lower the spinning mark has been set on the gauge, the greater the bite will be. Finally, with the water becoming quite low, if falls below the level that signals 'fly-only'. The trouble is that fly rods are covering only the last of the 'possibles' with any chance of a fish and failing miserably on the 'impossibles'.

You may think this far-fetched, but I think it is the basis of the "Oh-the-fly-doesn't-do-well-here," attitude present on so many of the 'any-method' rivers. And if I am right in my suspicions about the range from 'almost definites' through to 'impossibles', all I can say is that you can hardly expect the fly to work unless you are prepared to try it. I am reminded of those who mock a new technique, or a new pattern, but never think to try it until all else has failed. "There, I told you it was no bloody good!" is the comment, despite the fact that nothing else has worked either.

A middle Tweed beat in October or November may cost several thousand pounds, and that will pay only for one rod. Rod, lines, reels, waders and accessories can see off another thousand, with a further large amount going on hotel and bar bills, gillie's tips and the like – unless the choice of fishing is on association water, and the choice of bed beneath the B&B sign. Either way, all the salmon will care about is the concoction of metal, plastic, floss, fur and tinsel that is swam across its nose. It is the fly alone that the salmon rejects or accepts. Of course, the way it is presented is important, but the pattern or design of fly cannot be without significance.

"Any fly, so long as it's a Willie Gunn on a 2-inch copper tube," I hear them say. Well up to a point! Once we have made the decision to fish a fly which we assume is a representation of the type of bait-fish that the salmon have preyed upon at sea, there is little point in fishing one any smaller. However, I am not one of those who is convinced that the only thing to be said in favour of a change in fly is to revive the flagging spirits of the fisherman, although that is a pretty strong argument for ringing the changes.

For me, those changes are based largely on the colour of the water. I use bold, bright patterns when the water is coloured, subdued patterns when it is clear, and ring the changes in between.

It was the late John Ashley-Cooper who said that a choice of yellow, orange, black, or a mixture of these, created the best wing for the long flies we associate with cold water. The Willie Gunn, with its mixed wing of black, orange and yellow over a gold-ribbed black body, conforms to this 'rule' and has emerged as perhaps the greatest of the modern cold-water alternatives. I am not alone in stating that I often fish with nothing else, but I do allow myself the latitude of varying the proportions of hair in the wing.

I have flies in which the yellow and orange are beefed up to the extent that no room is left for more than a few strands of black. This is a grand pattern for a coloured water. In clear water, on the other hand, the wing will be virtually all black. And besides the standard Willie Gunn, with its equal proportions of all three colours in the wing, for use when the water is falling and clearing (when most salmon are caught), I like a fly with equal parts of black and orange over a thin, but long, central core of yellow, with jungle-cock cheeks added.

But where my autumn flies differ markedly from those I use in spring is in their dashes of red. I do like to see red in my autumn flies, and not just in recognised patterns such as the Garry, which has red as a base to its yellow-orange wing. Yellow . . . that's another of my autumn foibles, for I look for an orangey-yellow and shy away from the lemon-yellow hair so often seen. Red I use also in its simplest form in the Black-and-red, one of our most successful patterns in clear, cold water. Experienced fishermen have known this for years. Red and black, mixed or in bunches, tied over a silver-ribbed black body, has long been a standard pattern.

Other patterns which I like for autumn include a variety of Whitewings, which show their best either in the lowering light of dusk, or when the first frosts have filled the river with leaves. Then there is the Comet, a really mixed-up fly. It has a yellow hackle or short, yellow hairwing above the tail. Above that comes a red section occupying half the length of the body, which is sheathed with a red wing; above that, a black section; and, finally, a long thinnish black wing that extends right down to the yellow tail. An alternative dressing incorporates a touch of orange.

So the list goes on. Black-and-yellow flies are heavily favoured on Tweed, and if you ask for the pattern in one of the better, local tackle-shops, such as Angler's Choice, in Melrose, or Forrest's in Kelso, you may asked to be more specific. The boatman on the Junction likes a mixed-wing version tied with four alternate bunches – black, yellow, black, yellow – and this variant is named after him. It catches a lot of fish, as it is the pattern he regularly suggests to fishing guests! Then there is the Half-and-half, and the Yellow Dog (which is definitely *not* the same fly as the Garry Dog). Many Tweed fishermen will choose one, and only one, of these yellow-and-black variants to the exclusion of all others.

I like my long flies to have a light body, but perhaps that needs clarification. It is not simply a matter of choosing a certain material for the tube or shank. Much depends on the design and profile of the fly. For example, tie a 1-inch wing on a 1-inch copper or brass tube, and it is undoubtedly a heavy fly. But tie a 3-inch wing on the same tube, and it is a relative lightweight in terms of its overall length. I like this style of fly. It has 'weight' without being heavy, and the weight is all in the right place to keep the fly swimming on an even keel.

Experience with really long-winged flies gives me great confidence to fish flies with wings that trail behind the hook. As a rough-and-ready guide, I like the wing to extend back about $1^1/_2$ times the combined length of the tube, or shank, plus the treble. Thus, given a 2-inch tube on which to tie a fly, I would allow an inch for the treble, and hand back a pattern with a $4^1/_2$-inch wing – which might not be what was wanted!

I like to think that such relatively light and weight-forward flies fish at or above the same level as the line. I refer to this as the 'balloon effect', likening the method of presentation to a child holding a balloon on a piece of string in a breeze. My line is the child, the leader is the string, and the light fly represents the balloon as it darts, weaves and hovers. This, to my mind, creates a far better stimulus to a salmon than a heavy, dull and lifeless fly fished off a slow-sinker. So I fish rather faster-sinking lines, shorter leaders and lighter flies than most salmon-fishers. The reason for the short leader, sometimes as little as 4 ft, but never more than 7 ft, is that having gone to the bother of casting and controlling a fast-sinker, I do not want to let my fly fish *too* far above it.

Thinking again about the short tube or shank with a long wing, I could, of course, simply choose a lighter but longer tube, replacing copper with, say, plastic. But that would give the fly the same tendency to swim on an even keel. Conversely, if I want a heavier fly, to be fished in a stronger stream, where weight distribution is less important, I increase the tube- or shank-length, but maintain the wing-length up to the point where I am fishing the conventionally proportioned fly.

The pursuit of depth can be a fascinating concept, so, I hope I will not ruffle too many feathers when I say that I suspect that most of us are guilty of standing it on its head. Perhaps it is all this talk about sinking rates, expressed in so many inches per second, that makes us think and talk in terms of depth below the surface. You know the sort of thing: "I like to have my fly fishing 2 ft down in cold-water conditions."; or "There's seldom any need to fish your fly deeper than 3 ft below the surface".

What we should really be talking about, surely, is height above the river-bed? I would far rather hear comments such as: "You don't need to be scraping the bottom,"; or "So long as you can fish your fly within a couple of feet of the river bed. . ." I don't think I'm being foolish in suggesting that cold-water tactics are concerned with swimming the fly close to where the salmon are resting, rather than taking the fly to a predetermined depth.

Salmon lie in water of all depths and speeds, particularly in autumn. We must take this into account when determining tackle and tactics for the day. The solution is sometimes quite simple. Consider an 'average' pool on a 'standard' river, with fast, shallow water in the neck, slackening and deepening into the dub, and then becoming shallower and accelerating steadily through the glide and into the tail.

We may only need one combination of sinking line and fly to fish this pool effectively throughout its length, and in realising what we are trying to achieve, we should avoid mistakes.

In the headstream, because the water is fast-flowing, we will cast at a shallow downstream angle, with a long line, throwing a quick upstream mend as the line alights on the water, keeping the rod pointed toward the opposite bank, and perhaps wading deeply, thus doing everything we can to fish the fly as slowly as possible to give it time and scope to sink to a good fishing depth. The depth may be little more than 18 inches in a truly fast stream, but then the stream itself is barely more than 3 ft deep in the area we are covering, so the fly should be close enough to any potential taker resting on the river-bed.

The water is slacker down at the dub of the pool, so we start casting at a much squarer angle, even though we may shorten line slightly now that it is easier to cover the water with our squarer cast. We dispense with the mend (it's a nuisance, anyway), but then we start to lead the line and fly across with the rod, because we are getting a little impatient. And, of course, because the water is so much deeper, we have edged our way inshore.

My goodness! No wonder the spinner can beat the fly-fisherman hands down! For what we have done is to combine everything known to man to ensure that our fly fishes fast and shallow rather than deep and slow. We may have achieved the same depth of 18 inches that we had up in the stream, perhaps a few inches more, but we have ignored the obvious point that water-depth has increased to at least 6 ft. To get our fly swimming within 2 ft of the fish, we should have been getting line and fly at least 4 ft below the surface. We should have continued with our long, shallow-angled casts, using the mend and pointing the rod across the stream, and so on. The only facet we might have avoided would have been the wading.

Having done all this, we now find that the deeply-sunk line is an absolute beast to bring to the surface. Nothing beats a long rod for what comes next. Raise the rod to the vertical and roll-cast, and perhaps do it again to get the line up. Then go into whatever cast you please, but, for my money, unless a strong upstream wind is blowing, it will be the double-Spey. This is far and away the safest cast to use where sinking lines and big flies are being used.

Increasing water-depth creates ever-greater problems for the fly-fisher. Over a certain depth, either things become totally impossible or else you weary of the sheer hard work of roll, roll and perhaps roll again, and then Spey-cast. This is where we would normally reach for a spinning rod – but remember it's fly-only on the Tweed after mid-September.

The alternative is to use the shooting-head, which, although it is within the *legal* definition of fly-fishing, is in my view spinning with a fly-rod. But despite my prejudice, I readily acknowledge that the shooting-head provides perhaps the most effective method, possibly the only method, of fishing some of the darkest, deepest and most mysterious dubs on Tweed.

The tackle is as straightforward as it is coarse. The rod is likely to be the most powerful 15-footer you can lay hands on – a really tough, beast of a rod, and the reel a large-diameter but narrow-spool model. Load the reel with heavy mono backing and then your choice of shooting-line (non-tangle, flat-sectioned mono is popular), leaving just enough room for 12-15 yds of sinking line. If you cut a double-taper line of standard length exactly in half, you'll have two shooting-head lines, each measuring 13½ yds. And let's not beat about the bush, we'll choose an AFTM 12 ultra-fast sinking line. (I absolutely refuse to use a lead-cored line, but you might talk me into thinking about one of those deep-water-express-whatsits.)

So now we have rod, reel and two spools loaded with shooting-heads of various sinking rates. Needle-knot 18-inch lengths of 30 lb nylon to the points of the heads to take 5 ft leaders attached loop-to-loop. The leader should never be less than 20 lb breaking strain. I will tell you why in a moment.

The flies used will be tubes, normally copper or brass, because the emphasis is on achieving depth. They may be tied fairly thin in the wing to maximise their weight-to-surface-area ratio and to cause them to sink faster. They should be garish patterns for high water, and of more subtle tones for clear water.

The use of a shooting-head dictates an overhead cast. At the end of the back-cast, the heavy tube-fly will be speeding like a bullet. Then it comes to a dead-stop as you start the forward throw. This puts a considerable strain on the leader, and that is why I suggested a minimum breaking strain of 20 lb. Anything lighter might snap, or at least be seriously weakened. Oh, yes, there are just two more requirements for this style of Tweed fishing: it does help to have a boat and boatman. A boat provides a casting platform, and with many yards of running line to be retrieved before each cast, the problem when wading is what to do with it. Reservoir fishermen use line-trays, but the bottom-boards of a well-maintained boat, free of nails and splintered wood, provide a much better surface on which to coil line.

So there you sit, in the stern of a shallow-draft Tweed boat, looking rather bossy on your revolving stool, while the boatman plies the oars. He will, if necessary, tell you the angle and distance at which to aim, and with the shooting-head just beyond the tip ring of the rod, and a measured amount of running line coiled at your feet, you will do as you are bid.

Concentrate on keeping the line as high as possible on both back and forward casts. One serves to reassure the boatman that he is not likely to end up with a Willie Gunn ear-ring. The other serves to aim the shooting-head high and give it maximum scope to rocket out over the water, pulling the shooting-line in its wake.

Wishing your fly, leader, shooting head and running line *bon voyage*, you can settle back to survey the surrounding scene. Your boatman may mutter instructions as to the angle at which your rod should be pointing, and if you are perceptive to such things, you will be aware that his constant rowing is not only holding the boat into the current, but also crabbing it across the stream. This could, I suppose, be likened to harling, as practised on the Tay, where it works surprisingly well, except that they cheat by using three rods instead of one.

"Right then! Bring it up!", says the boatman, and you start to retrieve and coil the shooting-line until the head is up to the rod-tip, by which time the boatman will have manoeuvered the boat to the next casting position.

"Aye, same length and angle," he says, and on you go . . .

Your boatman may suggest that you should try giving the fly plenty of time to get down really deep, and then just twitch it back through the depths. Later, he may suggest a change of fly from his original choice.

One thing is for sure: if taking fish are in the deep dubs, this tackle and technique will find them out. When one takes, you'll discover that, contrary to Spey practice, where the boat is headed straight for the shore for you to 'shuffle-bottom' over the stern and play the fish off the bank, a Tweed boatman often prefers to stay out in the river for rather longer. When he does take the boat ashore, you will be instructed to stay on your stool. If he has miscalculated, and the salmon finds a reserve of energy for a long, downstream run, he will hop back in the boat and set off after it.

Finally, out comes the big net, carried in every Tweed boat and looking as if it came from the local blacksmith's rather than a tackle-shop, and the salmon is safely bagged. You can get out of the boat now, and join your man on the bank. Offer him a good stiff dram to celebrate the fish, because he has earned one. Oh, and pour one for yourself. But don't waste too much time. With salmon to be caught, the boatman is ready to push off, this is a great way of killing them.

Now let us look at rather shallower waters, perhaps on upper Tweed, one of its tributaries, or over on a Solway river such as Annan or Nith.

The river is running high, but it has fallen and cleared nicely after an enormous spate, and the pools are in perfect ply. The whole scene spells 'fish'. We walk down to the head of an excellent-looking stream.

In low water, this stream would be no more than 1-2 ft of quite slow-moving water over gravel. The only deepish water, about 3 ft at normal levels, is in the fairly narrow channel hard in on the opposite bank. However, with 2 ft showing on the gauge, the stream has risen to about 3 ft, deepening slowly, then dipping down into the rock-strewn channel over which there is about 5 ft of water.

The flow doesn't look particularly strong, but step into it in your waders and you realise its force. Even so, you reckon you've made the right choice in keeping to a slow-sinker and 2-inch copper-bodied tube-fly. The leader is 6 ft of 15 lb nylon and you are using a 15 ft carbon rod a nice outfit with which to cast and fish, and not too heavy.

Starting at the head of the stream, you let the stream draw out some 15 yds of line and then make your first cast. When its fished out, you draw two more yards off the reel but stay where you are and make another cast. And so you stay in the same spot, lengthening line by 2 yds at each cast until you have out what you feel is a comfortable length. If it is not enough to allow you to cast at a fairly shallow angle and still pitch your fly close to the opposite bank, then you have the option either of wading a little deeper or striving to put out a few more yards of line.

When fishing a sinking line, I like to be able to peep through the last few coils of line on the reel to see the join with the backing. This means that I am fishing with about 25 yds of line which, with a sinker and 15 ft rod, is neither too difficult nor too easy to achieve. This length of line allows the fly to fish slowly across its arc. If I feel the need to cast further, rather than busting a gut on the 15-footer, I change up to my 17-footer. This puts casting ranges into another league, particularly if using the double-Spey cast in a steady downstream wind. And this means a 35 yard line is needed.

In this press of stream, you certainly see the need to throw in one big, upstream mend, which should allow the fly to cut down into the water over the channel. In fact, this may be the main worry – that the fly is not getting deep enough. Having fished down the stream once with the slow-sinker, you may like to fish it down again with a faster-sinking line. Meantime, holding back a yard or two of the line you are shooting will allow you then to pitch it out to create a bigger upstream mend. And take your downstream pace after, rather than before, you cast. In the few moments of 'drift' caused by a combination of these two 'wrinkles', the line and fly may gain an extra foot in depth.

On you go. Roll the line up to the surface, double-Spey cast, throw a big mend and take a pace downstream. You'll not need to touch the line until it has swung round on to the dangle. Even then you can leave it alone, for the water downstream is fast enough to work the fly attractively. Now start to raise your rod-tip and lead the fly across. You are wading fairly deep, so fish may be lying below you, or a hesitant fish may have followed the fly across.

The reason for raising the rod is two-fold. Bringing it across in a near vertical semi-circle avoids two things. First, if you simply swing the rod round on the horizontal, the fly drops back in the stream. On a 15 ft rod, the fly would fall back 15 ft. Also, fish are notoriously difficult to hook securely when they take on the dangle. To point the rod straight down the line at them increases the risk of the hook pulling out, or of it tipping the fish on the nose. A nose-tipped salmon will come creaming up to the surface and lash about in a shower of foam until it throws the hook. A high-held rod, on the other hand, creates 'droop' in the line, which gives the salmon scope to turn while it is straightening. Also, the high rod acts as a cushion to the take. I have described all of this before, but it bears repeating for the extra salmon it brings safely to the bank.

Three casts later, the line suddenly stops in its swing. You have barely noticed this before the reel *clicks, clicks* again, and the line is torn away. Stay calm. Right! Now clamp the line and raise the rod. A short but hard fight, and 10 lb of silver salmon is in the net. It's another success for the salmon fly in autumn.

Hooking technique has been the source of as many arguments over the years as any other aspect of salmon-fishing you may care to mention. The controversy seems to hinge on whether or not slack line should be fed to a taking fish. Some say let everything go slack when a salmon takes. Others say the fish should be hit as soon as it's felt. My own position, which is on the middle ground, is attacked from both sides!

First, lets consider summer salmon and grilse. They are normally encountered in relatively fast water, or else we are adding considerable movement to the fly, and usually they take positively.

If your choice of flies is similar to mine, you will be fishing with small, needle-sharp and fairly fine-wired doubles and trebles. The fly will swim steadily across the river on either a floating or intermediate line. Up jumps the line, down dips the rod-tip and, before you have time to think, a salmon is on. With the hooks being used, what possible argument can there be not to set the hook immediately?

Later in autumn, as in spring, we fish larger flies, deep and slow, which does little to produce a positive take. The salmon are a little slower in turning and hooking themselves. There you have it in a nutshell: leave it to the salmon to hook themselves and you won't go far wrong.

I have never actually seen the take of a salmon in deep, cold water. So far as I am aware, nobody has. I do, however, try to interpret the messages telegraphed up the line. Such tentative conclusions as I have been able to make lead me not to feed *slack* line to the fish, but to allow it to take line against a *light tension* by setting the reel drag to the absolute minimum required to prevent an over-run.

A salmon takes and the reel clicks or purrs into action. I do absolutely nothing. Next the reel brakes into song, perhaps even screams, and yards of line are torn away. Now I clamp the line and raise the rod. All other things being equal, the salmon is mine. Some gillies say you should wait until the reel has stopped screaming before tightening. Many fishermen, until they have confidence in the technique, bring up their rods as soon as it has started! Personally, I hear the *click* and the *purr*, wait a second or three after the scream starts, and then tighten. This seems to work as well as anything.

Let me offer you an analogy, even though it may not be a good one. Let me rig up a rod with line, leader and fly and pull out, say, 20 yds of line. Now, pretend your hand is a salmon's mouth. Turn your hand so that it is palm downwards, and then bring your finger-tips together so that they all rest on top of your thumb. Now take hold of the fly with your fingers pointed toward me, and the treble hook resting between the ball of your thumb and the palm of your hand.

If I now give a sharp tug on the line, you will swear loudly and one of three other things will also happen. The first possibility is that a hook will drive into the palm or your hand or the ball of your thumb. The second is that the fly will jump forward and the treble will catch you in the finger-tips. The third is that you will manage to open your fingers in the nick of time and the fly will pop out of the trap.

Equating that to fishing, we may, on a one-out-of-three chance, hook a fish securely by hitting it the moment it is felt. The next possibility (which in my opinion is the most common) is that the salmon will be tipped in the nose or at the front of its mouth, which gives a notoriously bad hold. The third and least likely possibility (at least when a treble is used) is that we will miss the fish entirely.

What if we feed slack? Many fishermen hold a yard or two of slack line and let it go as soon as they feel a fish take. I would make two points here. First, if you have felt the fish, then presumably the fish has felt, and may already be trying to spit out the fly. If so, feeding slack can only help it. The method also relies on the assumption that the fish will push the fly up to the roof of its mouth with its tongue as a prelude to swallowing. But if we accept the premise that a salmon does not feed in freshwater, why should we presume that it is doing anything but a 'smash and grab' on the fly? We can put hand on heart and say that the salmon has *gripped* the fly, but that is about as far as we can go. So back to your hand with the fly in it. . . .

The general pattern of a salmon's take involves it moving forward and up, to varying degrees, to intercept the fly. We hope that it will then turn with the fly and return to its lie. I will consider a little later the salmon that doesn't turn.

So, turn your hand and start to walk away from me. Line starts to run off the reel, and if you are holding the fly lightly, or try to let go of it, you will feel it turning, and the hook will soon be burrowing into the triangle of flesh that separates your thumb from your index finger. If you hold the fly tightly and keep walking, however, you will have just as long as I care to give you before I clamp the line, raise the rod, and set you off cursing and swearing again. And the hook will be in that same triangle of flesh which, in salmon terms, would be right back in the scissors – the securest hook hold of all.

How secure *is* a hook-hold? If you have a faint stomach, skip the next paragraphs. I was sorting through my flies when I noticed that some of the larger, wire-shanked types had been made up (by myself, incidentally) with rather stiff extension tubing in a style exactly similar to a double Waddington shank in its hook attachment. Basically, you slip some extension tubing over the eye and down the shank of a treble, clip the treble on to the bottom loop of the shank, then pull up the extension tube so that it covers the eye of the hook and the loop of the shank. It's simple and straightforward, and if the hook is damaged, you simply push the extension tube back on to the hook-shank, and slip it off the loop and attach another treble. Yes, it's simple and straightforward *unless* the tubing you are trying to push back is hard and resistant.

You've guessed the rest! I tried to lever at the tube with my thumbnail and just as I was thinking, "This is a bit dangerous", my thumb slipped and one point of the size 4, extra-strong, out-pointed Rob Wilson treble was embedded right up to its bend in the bed of my thumbnail. The next thing I knew, I was holding the fly in one hand, and sucking the thumb of the other.

Carolyn looked up from the papers. "Did you stick a hook in yourself just then?" she asked.

"No dear, just sucking my thumb."

I had simply pushed down on the barb-side of the hook to enlarge its entrance channel, and pulled. This is a minor operation I have done, seen done, or had done, on several occasions, the first being to extract a treble from the ball of my thumb. The gillies on the Lochy made a great thing of it, offering me "A dram for the pain if the flesh tears," one of them pinning my arm on the car bonnet while the other took my thumb in his paws before turning

HOOKING THE SALMON OF AUTUMN

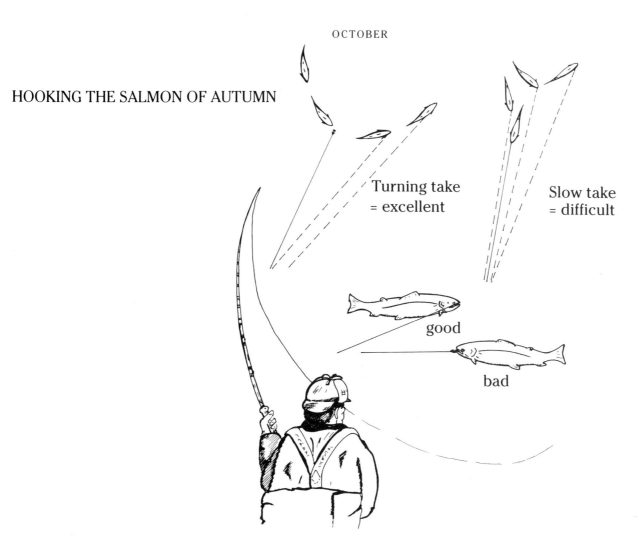

Turning take
= excellent

Slow take
= difficult

good

bad

Leading the fly positively across the dangle by leading with a high rod point

his back on me. Then he turned, saying, "It's no good. You'll have to away to the hospital!" I was remonstrating that it would be a waste of good fishing time before I noticed their silly grins and that I had no hook in my thumb!

So, be careful with hooks, and always use the most pliable extension tubing you can find, be it on a tube, wire-shank or Waddington. And remember, if I can pull out a fly-hook so easily, with just a little bit of leverage, then so can a salmon.

I mentioned earlier that some salmon either refuse to turn in the take or turn late. It is possible to differentiate, although the signs are difficult to describe. It seems that the fly swims in front of the fish, which, its curiosity aroused, either swims forward to the fly or tracks along behind it and *then* comes forward. Either way, it simply sucks the fly in and drifts back with the current, neglecting to turn. I deduce that this is what happens from the messages at the reel – no shrieks or screams, just clicks, purrs and then sighs. Either way, whether the salmon has returned to its lie or is perhaps in process of turning, the only thing to do is to raise the rod gently and 'feel' for fish. If pressure increases and the reel starts to chatter, you clamp the line and tighten.

Let's hope that this autumn produces fish that turn well in the take. On shallower stretches, when fish rise up and through the fly, they may even bulge or break the surface. The line jumps and the reel sings before you tighten, and then comes that indescribably 'electric' throbbing as the fish pulls against the spring of the rod. When a salmon takes like this, turning as it goes, everything happens so cleanly that no doubt is left as to whether the hook is well set. As I have said elsewhere, long-winged patterns, by they full-blown versions such as the Collie or semi-long, like my favoured 1¹/₂-inch shank and treble with a 3-inch wing, do tend to produce fish that turn well in the take.

Finally, it has to be said that the method of allowing a salmon to take line off the reel under light tension depends on no line having been retrieved before the take. Line may have been drawn in to maintain the water speed of the fly across a slack section of the river or because the fly has been on the dangle and is being drawn up both to tempt a following fish and in preparation for the next cast. What then? Well, if it is one of those days when I am feeling particularly calm and collected, and I almost *sense* the fish taking before I feel the tug. Then I let it take the slack, running it through my fingers under light tension. But a sudden tug leaves no room for subtleties, and I up with the rod and give it 'a good bash'. Now you know why I pray for fish that turn positively in the take and *before* I have started hand-lining!

THE ESSENTIALS OF AUTUMN

Flies: Many fishermen, once the water temperature has fallen below 45 degrees, take the attitude of "any fly, so long as it is a 2-inch Willie Gunn", and put their thoughts and efforts into fishing this one fly effectively. There are alternatives, however, which may do more than simply revive the flagging spirits of a fishless fisherman. The general rule is to use bright, bold patterns when the water is high and coloured, and smaller, subdued patterns when the water is clear. Local tackle-shops on Tweedside or on the Solway rivers should put you right.

Tweed favourites include the Black-and-yellow in a number of styles, Black-and-orange, Black-and-red, Yellow-and-orange, Garry Dog, Yellow Dog, the Comet, various Whitewings and, of course, the Willie Gunn and its half-brother, the Munro Killer. All these would be tied upon articulated shanks – tubes, Waddingtons or Brora-style shanks – and armed with a treble hook. However, when a lot of leaves are in the river, or gravid fish that the sportsman will wish to return alive, the old-fashioned single salmon iron can still have its day.

Lines: The choice of line depends on the depth of water. On shallower streams on Solway rivers, upper Tweed and its tributaries, an intermediate or slow-sinker may be sufficient. Normally, a fast-sinker such as the Wet-Cel 2 will cope with deeper water, fished in a full-length double-taper with a combination of roll- and Spey-casts. However, on the deep dubs of lower Tweed, which are often fished from a boat, fast-sinking shooting-heads are often used. Such lines require a long, powerful rod.

CHAPTER ELEVEN

November

THE SUCCESSFUL FISHERMAN

The successful fisherman is concentrating all the time on catching salmon. He is convinced that if a fish is there for the taking, then he will have it. He is thinking, breathing, smelling salmon. All other thoughts are put out of his mind. He has the competence, confidence, concentration, conviction and determination to succeed.

N ovember can be one of the busiest times of my fishing season both on Nith, which is on my doorstep, and Tweed, which is just a short drive away. On both rivers, the last to close in Scotland, salmon fishing goes on right to the end of the month. Yet, despite the hustle and bustle of the Borders' harvest time, I have often started looking back over the season, and doing some stocktaking, even before the month is out.

Some of my memories of fish, fishing and fishermen, will concern an aspect of my fishing year which so far has gone unmentioned. I run casting and fishing courses, give demonstrations and talks. After I had been doing this for a while, I realised that certain questions were cropping up time after time. One most-often repeated, in this age when available salmon fishing is hardly enough to go round, is how to gain access to good fishing. I always leave the questioner in absolutely no doubt that the only short-cut may lie in the status of his bank account, but usually I am able to set him off to search in some of the more likely directions.

A whole series of other questions, looked at objectively, all demand the same answer. They can be summarised as, "What makes a successful salmon fisherman?"

But before I go any further, let me offer one important apology, not to fishermen, but to all fisherwomen. I am aware that in my writing I tend to place emphasis on the male gender, by using what some may see as the old-fashioned term 'fisherman'. It is intended, of course, not only in the masculine but as an all-embracing term.

"So what?" some males may ask. Well, in choosing the title, 'The Successful Fisherman', for this chapter, I am only too aware that, taking their minority status on the riverbank into account, fisherwomen are, on the whole, more successful than their male counterparts when it comes to catching salmon. Make no mistake about it! Men outnumber women on the riverbank probably by a ratio of about 100:1, which is not reflected by their placings in the record lists. Georgina Ballantyne, who caught the British record salmon, is the shining light.

THE SUCCESSFUL SALMON FISHER SHOULD STUDY THE WATER CAREFULLY BEFORE DECIDING UPON TACKLE AND TECHNIQUE. HE WILL THINK ABOUT WATER AND OVERHEAD CONDITIONS, AND HOW THESE MAY EFFECT THE SALMON'S TAKING BEHAVIOUR.

But her success, by harling, may not be as significant as Mrs Robertson's British record for a salmon taken on fly. I wonder how many salmon-fishers are aware of the proportion of women who have the biggest fish or the most fish from various fisheries or beats?

A lesson is to be learned here, and it is the greatest lesson we will ever receive on our road to becoming successful salmon fishermen. It is parallel with the reason men have consistently emerged as top chefs in what is traditionally a female domain: the will to succeed, the determination to catch fish.

That, in my opinion, is what sets a successful salmon-fisher, male or female, apart from his fellows. It is the will to succeed, the determination to catch fish.

Determination to catch fish? But, surely, we all want to catch fish? Yes, but we are not all determined to do so. There lies the difference.

When people come to me for casting and fishing instruction, I reckon this, in itself, expresses a certain level of determination. What I presume they are really saying to me is, "Help me to enjoy the sport more, and to catch a few more fish".

My reaction is to take them back to the basics. Successful salmon fishing needs to be built on firm foundations. The first step is to choose appropriate tackle. This is the point from which we set off on the road to fishing with maximum efficiency and effect for the minimum of effort.

Few people do not have to operate within a more-or-less fixed budget. For the newcomer to salmon fishing, the first hurdle is the initial and unavoidable capital investment in rod, reel, lines and the general paraphernalia of the sport. The effort must be made to choose wisely. I would suggest that, at 1990 prices, a potential salmon-fisher can kit himself, or herself, out with one rod, one good salmon reel with a spare spool, and a floating line and a sinker, for about £300. The 15-footer is an excellent rod with which to learn and perhaps continue the craft of salmon fishing. You could pay more. You might pay less and come to regret it.

The next largely unavoidable expense is the purchase of a pair of chest-waders. These are far more appropriate to a salmon fisherman than thigh-waders, and should be viewed as a 'must' on all but small streams. Another 'must' is that they should have studded or felt soles to give grip on the river-bed. Do try them on in the shop. I am not sure whether Far Eastern manufacturers can't come to terms with the size of western bodies, or whether they are simply determined to reduce material costs to a minimum, but some of their chest-waders are little more than trouser-waders that come barely above the waist. And, if you intend to fish fast-flowing rivers with uneven beds, make yourself a wading-stick. It does not need to be anything fancy. A broom handle of about 5 ft will do nicely, with a lanyard at the top and heavily weighted with lead and shod with a rubber cap such as is used on some walking-sticks at the bottom. Used sensibly, this should keep you safe when you need to wade deep.

It is in the choice of leaders and flies that I am often amazed at some folk's penny-pinching attitudes. They have spent close to £400 so far, but now hesitate over paying the few pounds or pennies more that make the difference between top-quality or second-best nylon and hooks for their flies. I could buy cheaper nylon than the Bayer Perlon that I choose, but how would I feel when a 20-pounder took off on its first sizzling run? I was tempted in my student days to buy cheap hooks. They broke or straightened in fish – those, that is, that weren't rejected because of twisted eyes or shanks or, a common fault, doubles splayed too far apart. Eventually, I threw them all away. I would have saved money, and given a greater expression to my determination to catch fish, if I had bought top-quality hooks in the first place.

The willingness to ensure that all your tackle is more than adequate to cope with anything you may expect from it is a measure of your determination to succeed. Thinking 'fish' all the time will extend to taking care over details. The successful fisherman not only learns the best knots, but replaces his leader at the start of each fishing and after each fish he catches. If he sees a wind-knot in his leader, he does not say that it will do for another few casts. He replaces the leader because he is determined to hook a strong, lively salmon in the next few minutes. He will care for his reel, and ensure it is well oiled. He will tape his rod joints – particularly if he is a Spey-caster – and ensure that his reel is fixed firmly on the rod. He will check his hooks regularly, keeping the points needle-sharp, and rejecting any showing the first signs of rust – all because he is determined to catch fish.

Having bought his, or her, tackle, the man, or woman, who hopes to become a successful salmon-fisher will learn how to use it to his or her and the tackle's full potential. No, this is not a plug for my casting courses! It is an expression of my amazement at those who will spend a fortune on tackle, then pay the high costs of salmon fishing, but never think of investing a relatively small amount of time and money needed if progress from casting 15 yds of line to casting 30 yds. Salmon fishing with the fly is a craft, and it is built on choosing the right tools and learning how to use them. The man who is determined to catch salmon will recognise this as an inescapable fact.

Then comes the search for good fishing. It is said that a large part of successful salmon fishing depends on being in the right place at the right time. Some seem to think this is a matter of luck. Occasionally it is. Far more often, however, it is the result of determination to be there, which may bring a reassertion that success is measured by the depth of your purse. We are back to fixed budgets. But, in my opinion, a man who stays at an expensive hotel, runs up a big dinner and bar bill, and then can afford to fish no more than an overcrowded stretch of public water is not making the right choices if he wishes to catch more than an occasional fish. A determined fisherman will minimise his 'holiday' expenses so that he can 'maximise' the amount he can spend on fishing.

Having spent his money and made his choice, the successful salmon-fisher will then be determined to make the most of it. A story is abroad in certain fishing circles of a man who is a generous fishing host but who drives his guests so hard from dawn to dusk that they have been known to keel over, fast asleep, while up to the tops of their waders in the river! Most of us would agree that this is taking things a little too far. But the man who is determined to catch salmon will not do so unless his fly is in the water.

Fly-fishing for salmon has little to do with patience, but it does have a great deal to do with perseverance. My own approach is to keep ticking along, not pushing myself too hard because I know that I will need my reserves of energy when salmon are being caught, or when conditions suggest that they *should* be caught. Then, no number of wild horses could pull me away from the river-bank.

The man who is determined to catch salmon will resist falling into a stereotyped approach. Suppose he is faced with a big Spey pool, and suppose that conditions, with a water temperature of 50 degrees Fahrenheit, suggest that a floating line is appropriate choice of tackle. He has the pool to himself until lunchtime, when rods traditionally gather at the fishing hut for lunch and to be allocated their afternoon fishing. Looking at the length of the pool, he knows that if he takes one pace between casts, he will have just enough time to fish the pool once. He determines, therefore, to take three steps between casts, and so give himself the opportunity to fish the pool three times.

First time down, he may try a fairly large fly, fished off the floater. Second time down, he may try a smaller fly, or change to an intermediate line. Third time down, he could choose a 2-inch tube-fly fished off whichever sinking line will take it down to fish lying on the river-bed. By so doing he tries most of the available options, although, of course, if one of them works, then he keeps with it.

Now suppose it is earlier in the season, on the same pool, but with the temperature below the 50 degrees envisaged in the last example. First time down, he tries a sinker and a long fly, perhaps a Willie Gunn with a 4-inch wing. Second time down, he keeps to the same line, but tries a smaller fly, still a Willie Gunn, perhaps, or a Black-and-orange with jungle-cock cheeks. Third time down he tries a faster-sinking line and different design of fly or, if he is not a purist in such matters, he may put up his spinning rod.

The determined salmon fisherman is concentrating all the time on catching a salmon. He is determined that if a fish is there for the taking, then he will do all in his power to have it. He is thinking, breathing, smelling fish. All other thoughts are put out of his mind. How does he achieve this, when other, perhaps less successful, fishermen's minds are wandering off on to a hundred and one things?

In the February chapter, when I wrote about spinning, I mentioned the 3 Ds, depth, distance and dominance. Now, in terms of fishing effort and effect, I come to the 3 Cs: competence, confidence and concentration.

The determined salmon fisherman invests in appropriate tackle and takes the trouble to ensure that he is competent in its use. He is able to throw a long, but delicate and accurate, line using overhead, roll or Spey casts, as required, and he has learned how best to fish the fly. This gives him confidence, and because he is determined to do it well, he catches fish and his confidence grows because now he knows that he is getting it right. Little wonder, then, that he is encouraged really to concentrate on swimming his fly effectively and catching fish. Determined salmon-fishing is physically demanding, but it is also mentally stimulating and exhausting.

So there we have just a few answers to the question, "What makes a successful salmon fisherman?" It's as simple, and yet as complicated, as that.

THE SUCCESSFUL FISHERMAN

'Lord grant that I may catch a fish,
So big that even I,
In telling of it afterward,
May have no need to lie'

SUCCESSFUL SALMON FISHING HAS TO BE BUILT ON THE FIRM FOUNDATIONS OF CHOOSING GOOD TACKLE AND LEARNING TO USE IT TO FULL POTENTIAL – WITH MAXIMUM EFFICIENCY AND MINIMUM EFFORT.

OUTSTANDING SALMON FROM THE NITH – THE FRUITS OF A DETERMINED APPROACH TO FISHING. THESE SALMON WERE TAKEN ON A SPINNER BUT, ON TWEED, THE RULE IS 'FLY-ONLY' AFTER MID-SEPTEMBER.

SUCCESSFUL FISHERMAN'S CHECKLIST

● Start, continue and finish with the will and determination to succeed. Choose the best tackle that your budget will allow, but not necessarily the most expensive.

● Invest the necessary time and effort in proper instruction to ensure that your are using your tackle to something approaching its and your own full potential.

● Get the basics right. Concern yourself with the practical. Accept that salmon-fishing is more of a craft than an art or science.

● Spend your money wisely. The determined salmon fisherman will reduce his accommodation costs to allow himself to spend more on fishing rent.

● Pay attention to detail while you are fishing. If you are determined to catch fish, and expect one to take hold shortly, you learn to tie and use the best knots. If they do not snug down perfectly after you have moistened them with saliva, cut them out and start again.

● Replace your leader each day and after each fish, and check it regularly for wind-knots. If you find one, scrap the leader immediately. Never trust a suspect hook.

● Never fall into the trap of seeing the fishing of the fly as nothing more than a punctuation mark between casts. Good casting is enjoyable, but it should be recognised as nothing more than a means to an end.

● Relax when you are fishing. Never forget that you are there to enjoy yourself, and you can still do that even if you don't catch a salmon. But the determined and successful fisherman never enjoys himself quite so much as in that electrifying moment when he realises he is into a fish.

THE DETERMINED FISHERMAN

Getting down to some serious thinking about tackle and technique

CHAPTER TWELVE

December

AT SEASON'S CLOSE

Conservationists accept that populations of wild creatures need to be managed. They reject the protectionist or preservationist approach and accept that where a species is in surplus, a harvest can be taken, and all the better if this serves to create the interest and investment to conserve, enhance and nurture the status of the species and its environment. But we must, for the future, consider the salmon and our harvest of them not from the viewpoint of isolationists, but as one small part of a much wider picture.

December dawns, and there is no prospect of salmon-fishing, in Scotland at least, for more than a month. It's time to shop and prepare for the festive season. But, as Carolyn will be only to quick to tell you, I just cannot get salmon fishing out of my mind. Rods are checked, rings replaced if necessary, varnish touched up. I sort through my fly-boxes. With many gaps where favourite flies have been lost, or chewed to pieces by fish, I shall be spending time at the vice.

This sorting-out of flies allows me also to put them back in their boxes in some sort of order. I do like to know where to lay my hands on an Arndilly Fancy on a size 6 Esmond Drury hook when I want it.

Nevertheless, not too much should need to be done. I try, where my tackle is concerned, to follow the adage that "a stitch in time saves nine," and rely on running repairs throughout the season. Still, it is good to know what has gone missing, particularly if any of the family happens to as what I would like for Christmas this year? New rod-clips for my car roof . . . I must leave this page open.

But December has another aspect. In the last chapter, I wrote about starting to look back over the previous season. In December, one's thoughts turn to the future. It is not simply a matter of thinking about where and when I shall be fishing, nor whether or not I shall catch many, or any, fish. Longer-term thoughts will be about what the future may hold for the fish, for fishing, and for fishermen.

It doesn't need a mathematical genius to realise that the next century lies less than 10 years ahead. Perhaps my young sons lead me to think further ahead than I might otherwise.

JAMIE LITTLE, AT HOME WITH HIS FIRST SALMON. WE MUST ENSURE THE FUTURE FOR COMING GENERATIONS OF THE SALMON AND THE FISHERS. KING GEORGE VI EXPRESSED THIS CONCERN WHEN HE STATED: 'THE WILDLIFE OF TODAY IS NOT OURS TO DISPOSE OF AS WE PLEASE. WE MUST HAVE IT IN TRUST. WE MUST ACCOUNT FOR IT TO THOSE WHO COME AFTER.'

'RED IN TOOTH AND CLAW' THE PUBLIC WILL EXPECT WILD, NATURAL PREDATORS TO HAVE FIRST BITE AT THE CHERRY OF SALMON STOCKS – A SALMON'S FLANK FOLLOWING A CLOSE ENCOUNTER WITH A SEAL.

Or perhaps it is simply a determination to have and to hold, and to do anything I can to protect the future status of the wild species that I hold most dear. But I do spend a lot of time considering their future. Nothing is certain, except that we fishermen are those who must accept responsibility for the salmon, as well as the right to take a harvest from them.

The Salmon Bill is to me little more than a forlorn hope, a paper tiger, and now that the Government is turning its back on dealer-licensing, the whole thing may best be seen as a squandering of the public resoursces, and fishermen's time and effort. However, it has brought a greater recognition of salmon fishing as a vital part of many rural economies. It has created a climate in which efforts of rod-and-line interests to conserve salmon and improve rivers are more likely to gain the official nod of approval, and some of the recognition they deserve.

Thinking conservationists around the world accept that populations of wild creatures need to be managed. They reject the view of tunnel-visioned preservationists or protectionists, unless, as so often happens, a species is fighting for survival. Conservationists accept that a harvest may be taken from a species in surplus, and all the better if this creates the interest and investment to conserve, enhance and nurture the species and its environment.

In this context, we should try to see salmon and fishing not from the point of view of isolationists, but as part of a much wider picture. If the salmon is seen as a symbol of pure water, for example, its future may be secure, and the harvest continued.

Deciding who will get what share of the harvest is, from the salmon angler's point of view, moving in the right direction. But it is still something of a juggling act. For one thing, we may have to accept that public opinion will demand that natural predators, be they terns gorging on smolts or seals preying on returning, mature fish, will have first bite at the cherry. I have great sympathy with the attitude that says man should be part of rather than master of his environment. After that, I think we are free to limit any purely commercial harvest of salmon to leave more for rod-and-line interests.

I see this not as a dog-in-a-manger attitude, but rather as one which meets the needs of society. Beside the provision of recreation, a salmon taken on rod-and-line is worth about 70 times more to the economy than the income generated by the taking of the salmon in a net. And far greater numbers of people are employed, either directly or indirectly, as a result of rod-and-line fishing than any other section of salmon-based industry. Netsmen could be more gainfully employed in hatcheries, or river-improvement work, as gillies or keepers.

After that, we take the harvest but preserve the cherry-stone, or, rather, the necessary stocks of salmon in sufficient numbers to continue the species. To continue the species? Why should we not be doing everything we can to bring salmon rivers to peak production?

I have considered the views of informed conservationists. There is, of course, another side to the coin. Many people agree that because we eat what we catch, our sport is justified. Yet some folk suggest that we should return more, or all, of the salmon we catch, not simply kelts or gravid fish. Where does that lead us? It should be remembered that coarse fishermen return all the fish they catch, and take a lot of stick from the 'antis' as a result.

A recent invitation to me to appear on what might be described as a 'popular chat-show' was withdrawn at the request of the 'antis'. Their argument was not with me, as a salmon fisherman, they said, but with coarse anglers, and match fishermen in particular. But would they stop there? If match-fishing were banned, and then all coarse-angling, would they give us a smile and a wave?

If these are 'thin-end-of-the-wedge' tactics, if salmon fishing were to be banned, if fishermen were no more, who then would look after the salmon?